The Championship 1997

Football and Hurling

DEDICATED TO

TRISH, JOHN BRIAN, SARAH MARIE,

AND TO THE MEMORY OF MY BROTHER-IN-LAW, PAUL SHARKEY,

FROM ARDEE IN COUNTY LOUTH,

WHO SADLY DIED IN JULY OF THIS YEAR.

By the same author:
Football Captains 1940 - 1993
The Championship 1995 - Football and Hurling
The Championship 1996 - Football and Hurling

THE CHAMPIONSHIP 1997

FOOTBALL AND HURLING

The Complete Record

Brían Carthy

Published by
Sliabh Bán Productions Limited
Rathgar Villas, Dublin 6.

ISBN 0 9532236 0 4

A CIP record of this book is available from the British Library.

Cover Design: Mary Guinan, Temple of Design
Cover and colour photographs: Sportsfile
Layout and design: Mary Guinan
Printed in Ireland by Kilkenny People Printing

ACKNOWLEDGEMENTS

The author and publisher would like to thank all the people who assisted with the publication of this book. We would like to acknowledge the generous sponsorship of Eircell and thank especially their Sponsorship Manager Lisa Browne.

Special thanks also to Frank Greally, Michael Doherty, Danny Lynch, Mary Guinan from Temple of Design; to all our advertisers, and to the following for permission to use their photographs: Sportsfile, Oliver McVeigh, Brian Mulligan and Willie Donnellan.

Contents

MESSAGE FROM THE PRESIDENT

The increased popularity and profile of Gaelic Games in recent years has coincided with a welcome proliferation of GAA publications. These have covered virtually every aspect of the Association and our games. Until recently, however, there has been no comprehensive record of our Championships, recording details that would prove vital for future historians and students of our games. This omission has been redressed by Brian Carthy, commentator, broadcaster, analyst and aficionado of Gaelic Games.

Brian's passion for our games, his knowledge and his attention to detail is evident in his commentaries, Sunday after Sunday, through the medium of RTE Radio. In this record of the Championships he transfers his love of the games and his energies to produce the definitive record of 1997, speckled with gems of information and details obvious and relevant only when seen chronicled.

I would like to extend my gratitude and congratulations to Brian for his commitment, energy and initiative in producing another unique record of our Championships. I wish it well and hope that many more publications will emerge from his prolific pen in the new millennium.

Gur a míle maith agat agus rath Dé ar an obair.

Seosamh Mac Donncha,
Uachtarán,
Cumann Lúthchleas Gael

Introduction

1997 WAS THE YEAR when Kerry football once again took its place at the top table after eleven long years in the wilderness and the mighty men of Clare established themselves as the best hurling team in the land. It was a never-to-be-forgotten year in both codes! Maurice Fitzgerald, the finest footballer of his generation, finally got his hands on that elusive All-Ireland medal after a magnificent individual display in the Final. Fitzgerald exuded class and his nine points contribution ensured further misery for John Maughan's proud Mayo team.

Clare hurlers became giants of their time when they withstood a late Tipperary challenge to claim ultimate honours in a unique All-Munster, All-Ireland decider that was as tense and dramatic as it was close. Clare manager, Ger Loughnane, described it as "an epic, epic All-Ireland Final."

There were draws galore in football; more than the usual tantalisingly close finishes, some magnificent scores; joy and heartbreak in equal measure, and heroes and villains in every village and town in Ireland. And there were many, many glorious Sunday afternoons when football and hurling supporters travelled with a spring in their step and hope in their hearts to famous places like Croke Park, Semple Stadium, St. Tighearnach's Park, Tuam Stadium and all points in between.

It was at the Sports Field in Clonmel on Sunday, May 18, that a hurling goalkeeper, Brendan Cummins, stole the show at a football Championship game even though his name did not even appear on the match programme. Dual star Cummins was introduced as a substitute and scored eight points as Tipperary beat Limerick at the second attempt. And what about Martin Daly's exploits at Pairc Ui Chaoimh in mid-to-late June? Daly scored a sensational injury-time goal to give Clare their first Championship victory over Cork in fifty-six years. Incredible! But there was to be no fairytale ending for Clare as a wonder goal from flying wing-forward Pa Laide proved decisive as Kerry retained their Munster crown at the Gaelic Grounds in July.

West of the Shannon in late May, John Maughan's highly-motivated Mayo team beat Galway in a Championship game at Tuam Stadium for the first time since 1951. It was a momentous day in the North Galway town!

The highest individual score of Championship '97 was recorded by Declan Darcy, who scored 2-10 as Leitrim were somewhat fortunate to beat London after extra time.

Paul Taylor accounted for nine points as Sligo shocked Roscommon at Markievicz Park in the semi-final and came perilously close to causing a major upset in the Connacht Final when they scored 1-2 without reply in the closing stages. But time ran out - all twenty seconds of it - and Mayo held on to retain their title.

Offaly were the surprise packets of the '97 Football Championship as they regained the Leinster crown after a gap of fifteen years. Offaly scored 11 goals and 83 points in their six games in Leinster and the manner in which they disposed of reigning All-Ireland Champions Meath in the provincial decider must surely rate as the team performance of the year.

Earlier in the Leinster Championship, brave thirteen-man Kildare beat Laois but lost out to Meath in a compelling three-game semi-final saga that gave new meaning to the words courage and commitment. Meath had qualified to meet Kildare by virtue of a three points victory over arch-rivals Dublin in a game that set the Championship alight. It all came down to the last kick of the game and the Hill fell silent when Paul Bealin's penalty kick cannoned off the underside of the crossbar and Dublin were out of the Championship.

Cavan emerged from a twenty-eight-year wilderness to claim their 39th provincial title with a one-point victory over Derry in the Final. Mighty Stephen King collected the Anglo Celt Cup and Croke Park braced itself for Cavan's first Championship appearance in the 'theatre of dreams' since 1969.

Joe Brolly embarked on a kissing crusade in Ulster this year! And the cheekiest forward in the game scored three goals to underline his class. Gaelic Football is richer because of charismatic players like 'smiling' Joe from Dungiven!

Kerry qualified for their first All-Ireland Final since 1986 with victory over Cavan in the semi-final, while Mayo made sure of their place in Croke Park on 'big match day' by inflicting a six points defeat on Offaly.

The final itself was a celebration of the genius of Maurice Fitzgerald. Truly, the supreme artist!

•

IT WAS ANOTHER magnificent year in hurling, culminating with an unforgettable All-Ireland Final between Munster rivals Clare and Tipperary. Clare goalkeeper Davy Fitzgerald denied Tipperary victory in a pulsating encounter when he brought off a superb save from John Leahy late in the game. What a difference a save makes!

Clare began their campaign with a comfortable twenty-four points victory over Kerry at Cusack Park - a game in which wing-forward P.J. O'Connell scored 2-2 to demoralise the Kingdom. The Banner men had a much more difficult assignment against a highly-motivated Cork side in the next round when it took a late goal from substitute Stephen McNamara to ultimately decide the issue. On to mid-June where Tipperary signalled their Championship intentions with a ten points win over arch-rivals Limerick on a day when Michael Cleary scored 1-3 for the winners.

Substitute David Forde scored the only goal of the game as Clare defeated Tipperary in the Munster Final by three points on a 1-18 to 0-18 scoreline. Only the scoreboard disguised Clare's superiority!

Dublin hurlers ushered in the Leinster Championship in fine style with an emphatic sixteen points victory over a Westmeath team that failed to function on the day. Corner-forward Gerry Ennis scored an impressive 3-3 as the Dubs recorded the second-highest score of the Championship. On the same day at Cusack Park in Mullingar, a Johnny Dooley-inspired Offaly completely overwhelmed Meath in atrocious weather conditions. That victory set Offaly up for a semi-final meeting with Laois who tore the formbook to shreds with an astonishing second-half comeback that deserved a better result than a one point defeat.

DJ Carey made his entry into Championship '97 by scoring 1-7 as Kilkenny beat fourteen-man Dublin by seven points, while on the same day in Croke Park, Damien Fitzhenry pulled off a splendid injury-time save from Billy Dooley to put paid to Offaly's Championship aspirations!

Substitute Billy Byrne turned the Leinster Final decisively in favour of Wexford with a smash and grab 1-2 in the seven minutes he was on the field. Kilkenny joined age-old rivals Tipperary as 'back door' entrants to the All-Ireland quarter-final stages.

Galway had 37 points to spare over Roscommon in a totally lop-sided Connacht Final that will be remembered only for the serious head injury sustained by Joe Rabbitte. Noel Sands accounted for 1-9 as Down shocked Antrim in the Ulster Final but subsequently proved no match for beaten Munster finalists Tipperary in the All-Ireland quarter-final. In the second quarter-final, DJ Carey inspired a second-half Kilkenny comeback against Galway to clearly underline why he is the most outstanding forward in present day hurling. Carey scored 2-8 for what must surely rate as the finest individual performance of the Hurling Championship!

Jamesie O'Connor chose the All-Ireland semi-final to demonstrate his enormous talent and his nine points contribution paved the way for Clare's victory over Kilkenny, who became the first team to lose two Championship games in the one year! Tipperary, inspired by John Leahy, showed a vast improvement on their Munster Final performance to defeat the All-Ireland Champions, Wexford, by seven points.

Saffron-and-blue was the colour in Croke Park on Sunday, September 28, 1997, as Clare beat Tipperary for the second time in ten weeks to win a momentous All-Ireland Final. Another great day for the Banner county!

It was another wonderful year for hurling and football and I thoroughly enjoyed covering the games for RTE and meeting the many players, managers and all those who made such an enormous contribution to another memorable Championship season.

Brian Carthy

SUNDAY, SEPTEMBER 28, 1997

ALL-IRELAND SENIOR FOOTBALL FINAL

KERRY versus MAYO

CROKE PARK

REFEREE: BRIAN WHITE (WEXFORD)

RESULT: KERRY 0-13 MAYO 1-7

WHAT CAN ONE SAY! How about, thank God for Maurice Fitzgerald! Kerry's very own footballing genius turned in a superlative display that set him apart from all others on a day when Kerry claimed their 31st All-Ireland title with a three points victory over a disappointing Mayo side. All-Star Fitzgerald weaved his magic spell like no other and produced a performance of such rare quality that it must surely rate as one of the most outstanding individual displays ever witnessed on All-Ireland Final Day. Perhaps the best ever!

For far too long this modest son of Kerry soil was deprived an opportunity to showcase his incredible talent on Final day in Croke Park, but in the end the wait proved well worthwhile. The greatest and most naturally gifted footballer in the land decorated the greatest sporting day of the year with an array of skills that brought gasps of amazement from all sections of the 65,601 attendance in Croke Park and the millions watching worldwide on television. Cometh the hour, cometh the man.

Consider this! Fitzgerald scored no less than nine points and his kicking from play and frees was a joy to behold. But his final point of the game was simply out of this world! He kicked a wonderful long-range free out of his hands from the New Stand sideline to land his ninth point. It was fitting that the final act of the afternoon should produce such a stunning score from the master craftsman. It was the defining moment!

Many years ago George Best scored a spectacular goal for Manchester United. Old Trafford erupted. A young reporter enquired as to the time of the goal. An older journalist replied, "Never mind the time, son, just write down the date." Roll the clock forward to September, 28, 1997. Another genius, another code. Another spectacular score!
Never mind the time, but never forget the man. Maurice Fitzgerald. Simply the best! His name will forever be indelibly linked with the 1997 All-Ireland Football Final.

Fitzgerald's performance was all the more significant given the fact that he was involved in an accidental collision with his team-mate, Billy O'Shea, after just sixteen minutes play. The Laune Rangers player was forced to retire with a compound fracture of his ankle. Play was held up for nearly five minutes before O'Shea was transferred to the Mater Hospital in Dublin. It was cruel luck on O'Shea who had been very prominent before his unfortunate injury. By that stage, Maurice Fitzgerald had scored a point from a free but otherwise had hardly touched the ball. One wondered what thoughts were running through his mind when he saw O'Shea being stretchered off the field. It was clear he was upset to see his colleague in such pain. It was a real test of Fitzgerald's character and he rose to the challenge majestically.

O'Shea was barely in the ambulance when Fitzgerald landed a truly superb left-footed point from a free to push Kerry four points clear. John Crowley was called into the fray in place of O'Shea.

Pa Laide and Dara Ó Sé had scored the opening two points of the game as the Munster Champions took control from the very early stages. Mayo suffered a setback as early as the fourth minute when experienced corner back Dermot Flanagan had to go off injured to be replaced by James Horan, as John Maughan was forced to re-shuffle his team. But already a pattern was developing. Centre-half-back Liam O'Flaherty and midfielder Dara Ó Sé were establishing superiority early on, while Pa Laide was adding to his reputation with a fine display. William Kirby worked tirelessly to supplement Ó Sé's brilliance while, all round the field, Kerry won many of the personal duels.

Mayo continued to fritter away chance after chance from eminently scorable positions and 23 minutes had elapsed before the Connacht Champions opened their account through a long-range free from Maurice Sheridan. Kieran McDonald was suprised to see one umpire signal a point and another wave wide after fifteen minutes. Judging by his expression, the Crossmolina Deel Rovers player was certain he had scored Mayo's first point of the All-Ireland Final. But it was not to be!

Fitzgerald struck over a superb point from play after 25 minutes as Kerry tightened their grip on the game. Sheridan closed the gap with a pointed free, but Pa Laide replied for Kerry with a fisted point. Fitzgerald and Sheridan exhanged points to leave Kerry 0-7 to 0-3 ahead after 36 minutes. But it was noticeable that Sheridan was limping badly when he scored his third point and the Balla marksman was unable to re-appear for the second-half because of a hamstring injury. Liam McHale, out of sorts at full-forward, was moved to midfield late in the first-half, but Kerry finished the stronger with Fitzgerald kicking his fifth point to give the Munster Champions an 0-8 to 0-3 interval lead. Colm McManamon missed a gilt-edged chance of a score just before the half-time time whistle when he shot wide. It was symptomatic of Mayo's first-half performance.

Maurice Sheridan was replaced by Diarmuid Byrne at the start of the second-half as Mayo set about turning the tide. Kieran McDonald pointed from a close-in free to bring the Connacht Champions within striking distance. Mayo goalkeeper Peter Burke brought off a fine save, but there was little respite as Kerry continued to apply the pressure. Mighty Fitzgerald kicked two further points in quick succession; Burke deprived substitute John Crowley a certain goal with another splendid save, but inside a minute the Glenfesk man kicked a point from play to extend Kerry's lead to seven points. It was a scenario of nightmare porportions for the Connacht Champions!

By now the game had entered its most critical period! Kenneth Mortimer, James Nallen, Noel Connelly, Pat Fallon, Colm McManamon, Liam McHale and James Horan inspired the Mayo comeback. McManamon scored a fine point from play and then out of the blue came the goal that Mayo so badly needed. Seamus Moynihan was penalised for fouling substitute Diarmuid Byrne and Wexford referee Brian White awarded a penalty. Kieran McDonald scored a truly magnificent left-footed goal to change the course of the game. Now it was the turn of Kerry to experience the white heat of Final Day in Croke Park. Last year's All-Ireland Final hero, New Zealand-born, James Horan transformed the game when he kicked over two magnificent points to reduce the deficit to a single point! Mayo supporters roared their heroes on as Kerry appeared vulnerable. Fitzgerald and Hassett shot wide as Mayo sensed victory. But when the need was greatest, Fitzgerald once again delivered and his eighth point edged Kerry 0-12 to 1-7 ahead. The brilliant Peter Burke denied Denis O'Dwyer a certain goal while at the other end of the field Mayo spurned chance after chance. Kieran McDonald and P.J. Loftus were both off target from close range. John Maughan scratched his head in frustration. There is no doubt that Mayo had sufficient chances to win the game in the closing twenty-minutes but, not for the first time, appalling marksmanship put paid to their All-Ireland Championship ambitions. Kerry fought tenaciously in the closing tension-filled minutes to stave off resurgent Mayo and Maurice Fitzerald guaranteed his place in Gaelic Football folklore with a quite spectacular point with the last kick of the game to ensure Kerry their first All-Ireland title in eleven years. Truly, this was the Maurice Fitzgerald Final! A class apart!

SCORERS - KERRY: Maurice Fitzgerald 0-9; Pa Laide 0-2; Dara Ó Sé 0-1; John Crowley 0-1; MAYO: Kieran McDonald 1-1; Maurice Sheridan 0-3; James Horan 0-2; Colm McManamon 0-1.

KERRY

Declan O'Keeffe

Killian Burns — Barry O'Shea — Stephen Stack

Seamus Moynihan — Liam O'Flaherty — Eamonn Breen

Dara Ó Sé — William Kirby

Pa Laide — Liam Hassett — Denis O'Dwyer

Billy O'Shea — Dara Ó Cinnéide — Maurice Fitzgerald

SUBSTITUTES: John Crowley for Billy O'Shea; Donal Daly for William Kirby; Michael Francis Russell for Dara Ó Cinnéide

MAYO

Peter Burke

Pat Holmes — Kenneth Mortimer — Dermot Flanagan

Fergal Costello — James Nallen — Noel Connelly

Pat Fallon — David Heaney

Maurice Sheridan — Colm McManamon — John Casey

Kieran McDonald — Liam McHale — David Nestor

SUBSTITUTES: James Horan for Dermot Flanagan; Diarmuid Byrne for Maurice Sheridan; P.J. Loftus for David Nestor

KERRY

BACK ROW L TO R: Dara Ó Sé, Barry O'Shea, Liam O'Flaherty, Killian Burns, Billy O'Shea, Stephen Stack, Maurice Fitzgerald;
FRONT ROW L TO R: Pa Laide, Eamonn Breen, Seamus Moynihan, Liam Hassett, Declan O'Keeffe, Denis O'Dwyer, Dara Ó Cinnéide, William Kirby.

MAYO

BACK ROW L TO R: Liam McHale, Pat Holmes, Kieran McDonald, John Casey, Peter Burke, Pat Fallon, David Heaney, James Nallen, Maurice Sheridan;
FRONT ROW L TO R: David Nestor, Fergal Costello, Noel Connelly, Kenneth Mortimer, Dermot Flanagan, Colm McManamon.

SUNDAY, MAY 11, 1997

MUNSTER SENIOR FOOTBALL CHAMPIONSHIP PRELIMINARY ROUND

LIMERICK versus TIPPERARY

GAELIC GROUNDS, LIMERICK

REFEREE: NIALL BARRETT (CORK)

RESULT: LIMERICK 1-13 TIPPERARY 0-16 (A DRAW)

THE MEETING OF LIMERICK and Tipperary footballers generated little interest outside the confines of both counties, but the game itself at the Gaelic Grounds was highly competitive and gave the small attendance plenty to enthuse about. Limerick appeared on course for a surprise victory until teenager Declan Browne rescued Tipperary with a last-gasp equalising point to force a replay. Quite apart from landing the levelling score, Browne, once he settled down, had an impressive outing and emerged as top scorer with a tally of seven points.

Browne's only blot on his copybook was a missed penalty just coming up to half-time. When both teams met in a Division Three League game in February, Tipperary emerged victorious by three points, on a 0-9 to 0-6 scoreline. Tipperary had by far the better League campaign with three wins and a draw to their credit while Limerick's only victory came against minnows Kilkenny.

League form was set aside as a fit and eager Limerick team, favoured by a strong breeze, defied expectations and proceeded to dictate the pace from the throw-in by scoring the opening four points from John Quane, Derek Ryan, Donal Fitzgibbon and Pat Galvin. Although Quane and Donal Fitzgibbon held a distinct advantage at midfield, Limerick failed to take full advantage of the many opportunities that came their way and Tipperary came storming back to level the game at five points apiece. Peter Lambert and Derry Foley were prominent in that period of Tipperary dominance. Limerick fought back courageously in the closing minutes of the first-half with three unanswered points to carve out an 0-8 to 0-5 advantage at the interval.

Derek Ryan increased Limerick's lead shortly after the restart and they had stretched their advantage to five points by the end of the third quarter. It was time for cool heads and remedial measures by Tipperary. The impressive Browne answered the call with three points in quick succession. Derry Foley rowed in with another point and that was followed by two more from the elusive Lambert to edge Tipperary ahead for the very first time. The pendulum had swung in favour of Tipperary, but not for long. Outstanding Limerick midfielder John Quane showed commendable composure in crashing home the only goal of the game. Just reward for an excellent movement.

Tipperary responded again and a point each from John Owens and Brian Burke had the sides level for the third time.

Limerick substitute Noel Frewen rocked Tipperary with the lead point very late in the game before the assured and confident Browne, an All-Ireland minor hurling medal winner with Tipperary in 1996, landed the equaliser after latching on to a good pass from Peter Lambert.

Some days after the game, I spoke with a mightily relieved Tipperary manager Paddy Morrissey, who accepted his team were extremely fortunate to earn a second bite of the cherry.

"The selectors and myself couldn't wait for the referee to blow the full-time whistle when Declan Browne scored the equalising point. We were really glad to get out of the Gaelic Grounds with a draw. Limerick must be really upset that they didn't win the game. I hadn't seen Limerick play as well in ages, their midfielders were terrific. Our team didn't lift themselves on the day, especially our backs who played very poorly. Our midfielders also put in a terrible bad seventy minutes. Declan Browne and Peter Lambert brought us back into the game. We brought Brian Burke from full-forward to wing forward and that made a difference. Seán Collum had a terrific game as well after coming on for the injured Tom Anglim and he set up Declan Browne for the levelling point."

SCORERS - LIMERICK: Derek Ryan 0-5; John Quane 1-1; Pat Galvin 0-3; Damien Reidy 0-2; Donal Fitzgibbon 0-1; Noel Frewen 0-1 TIPPERARY: Declan Browne 0-7; Peter Lambert 0-4; Derry Foley 0-3; John Owens 0-1; Brian Burke 0-1

LIMERICK

	Richard Bowles	
Con Mc Sweeney	John Keane	Ger O'Connor
John Donovan	Tom Kelly	Denis Reidy
John Quane		Donal Fitzgibbon
Damien Reidy	John O'Halloran	Ed Walsh
Derek Ryan	Pat Galvin	John Conneely

SUBSTITUTE: Noel Frewen for Ed Walsh

TIPPERARY

	Martin Quinlivan	
Bernard Hahessy	Liam Cronin	Tom Anglim
Mark Sheahan	Brian Lacey	David Kennedy
Derry Foley		Christóir McGrath
Darren O'Connor	John Owens	James Williams
Peter Lambert	Brian Burke	Declan Browne

SUBSTITUTES: Seán Collum for Tom Anglim; Des Lyons for Darren O'Connor

LIMERICK

BACK ROW L TO R: Ed Walsh, Donal Fitzgibbon, John O'Halloran, John Quane, Richard Bowles, John Donovan, Tom Kelly, Derek Ryan;

FRONT ROW L TO R: John Conneely, Ger O'Connor, Denis Reidy, Con McSweeney, John Keane, Pat Galvin, Damien Reidy.

TIPPERARY

BACK ROW L TO R: James Williams, Brian Lacey, Christoir McGrath, Martin Quinlivan, Derry Foley, Brian Burke, Darren O'Connor, Mark Sheahan;

FRONT ROW L TO R: John Owens, Declan Browne, Peter Lambert, Liam Cronin, Tom Anglim, Bernard Hahessy, David Kennedy.

SUNDAY, MAY 18, 1997

MUNSTER SENIOR FOOTBALL CHAMPIONSHIP PRELIMINARY ROUND (REPLAY)

TIPPERARY versus LIMERICK

SPORTS FIELD, CLONMEL

REFEREE: NIALL BARRETT, CORK

TIPPERARY 1-17 LIMERICK 2-8

IT WAS THE DAY a hurling goalkeeper stole the show at a football Championship game even though his name did not even appear on the match programme. Dual star Brendan Cummins was only included in the Tipperary panel a few days before the game due to the unavailability of Peter Lambert, who was on honeymoon, and health concerns over Declan Browne, who scored seven points in the drawn game. Browne was hospitalised for a few days but recovered sufficiently to take his place in the starting line-up. The Moyle Rovers youngster scored four points before having to retire injured at half-time to be replaced by Cummins, who proceeded to showcase his undoubted talents as a footballer. With key forwards Lambert and Browne out of the picture, Cummins assumed responsibility in confident fashion and scored no less than eight points. Truly, a match-winning performance!

It had all begun so well for Limerick when their midfielder John Quane scored a fine goal after just fifteen seconds of play to stagger Tipperary. It turned out to be the fastest goal of the entire Championship campaign. Limerick were unable to build on that lead and it soon became apparent that Tipperary were superior in many areas of the field.

With Derry Foley and Seán Maher gaining plenty of possession at midfield, Tipperary battled back to level the game, courtesy of two points from Browne and one from the impressive John Owens. Limerick captain Ed Walsh edged Limerick ahead for the second and last time before Tipperary midfielder Maher scored the equalising point after fifteen minutes play. Then midway through the first half, centre-half-forward Owens scored a superb goal for Tipperary when he sent a powerful shot past Limerick goalkeeper, Richard Bowles.

Although Tipperary were now playing with a confidence that was rarely in evidence during the drawn game, their forwards failed to take advantage of the quality possession that came their way and they shot an unacceptable ten wides in the opening half. Despite the squandermania and the fact that Clonmel Secondary School student Browne struck the crossbar, Tipperary still led by three points, 1-6 to 1-3, at the interval.

Limerick full-forward Pat Galvin scored the opening point of the second-half to cut the margin to just two points.

Shortly afterwards, Tipperary goalkeeper Martin Quinlivan pulled off an excellent save to deny Limerick forward Derek Ryan a certain goal.

Tipperary had reason to be concerned at that juncture, but the game soon took a dramatic turn in their favour. Towering midfielder Derry Foley restored Tipperary's three points advantage, before substitute Cummins decided to make his mark on Championship '97. The Ballybacon Grange clubman helped himself to no less than eight points and played a vital role in consigning Limerick to the list of Championship also-rans for another year at least. To compound Limerick's misfortune, their captain Ed Walsh was ordered off near the finish following a second bookable offence. Late in the game, Tipperary goalkeeper Quinlivan blocked a penalty kick from Damien Reidy, but the Limerick half-forward scored a goal from the rebound for the final score of the afternoon. Certainly a day to remember for super-sub, Brendan Cummins!

SCORERS - TIPPERARY: Brendan Cummins 0-8; John Owens 1-1; Derry Foley 0-2; Declan Browne 0-2; Mark Sheahan 0-1; Brian Burke 0-1; Seán Maher 0-1; James Williams 0-1
LIMERICK: Damien Reidy 1-1; Pat Galvin 0-3; John Quane 1-0; Ed Walsh 0-2; Derek Ryan 0-1; Noel Frewen 0-1

TIPPERARY

Martin Quinlivan

Conor O'Dwyer | Niall Kelly | Liam Cronin
Seán Collum | Brian Lacey | Bernard Hahessy
Derry Foley | Seán Maher
Mark Sheahan | John Owens | Brian Burke
James Williams | Des Lyons | Declan Browne

SUBSTITUTE: Brendan Cummins for Declan Browne

LIMERICK

Richard Bowles

Con McSweeney | John Keane | Ger O'Connor
John Donovan | Tom Kelly | Denis Reidy
John Quane | Donal Fitzgibbon
Damien Reidy | John O'Halloran | Ed Walsh
Derek Ryan | Pat Galvin | John Conneely

SUBSTITUTES: Neilus Hunt for John Conneely; Noel Frewen for Pat Galvin

SUNDAY, JUNE 1, 1997

MUNSTER SENIOR FOOTBALL CHAMPIONSHIP

TIPPERARY versus WATERFORD

FRAHER FIELD, DUNGARVAN

REFEREE: WILLIE O'MAHONY (LIMERICK)

RESULT: TIPPERARY 2-7 WATERFORD 1-5

TIPPERARY ADVANCED to meet League Champions Kerry in the Munster semi-final with a none-too-inspiring display against a spirited Waterford side that hardly deserved to lose by five points. It was a boiling hot day at Fraher Field in Dungarvan, but the temperatures of the Tipperary supporters soared even higher as they watched their much-fancied team struggle to an unconvincing victory.

Favourites Tipperary only took the lead for the very first time with about thirteen minutes remaining when Brendan Cummins beat Waterford goalkeeper, Kieran Cotter, for a vital goal.

It was poor fare most of the way as both teams struggled to come to terms with the strong sea breeze which proved troublesome, especially for place-kickers. Cummins, who played in goal against Kilkenny in the National Hurling League the previous evening, had an uncomfortable afternoon and missed a number of scoreable frees until his second-half goal turned the tide firmly in favour of the Premier county.

Nothing came of Tipperary's early dominance as their forwards struggled to take advantage of the scoring opportunities that came their way. The Waterford defence marked tightly and goalkeeper Kieran Cotter dealt capably with everything that came his way.

Favoured by the breeze, Waterford opened the scoring with a fine point from Shane Bergin in the 12th minute and Gavin Keane extended their lead with a point from a free nine minutes later. It was very moderate fare until Keane produced a touch of real class. The centre-half-forward gathered a long delivery, totally outwitted Tipperary full-back Niall Kelly with a clever dummy and then drove the ball past Martin Quinlivan for a truly excellent goal. It was looking bleak for Tipperary when Keane added to his tally with a point to leave Waterford 1-3 to no score ahead after 27 minutes play.

But soon afterwards, a blunder by Waterford goalkeeper Kieran Cotter allowed Tipperary back into the game with the most fortuitous of goals. Cotter misjudged a speculative lob from midfielder Derry Foley and it bounced agonisingly over the keeper's head and into an empty net.

Cummins and the highly-impressive Keane swapped points before the referee called a halt to what was a mediocre first-half before an attendance of over two-thousand.

Tipperary's play improved significantly after the re-start and James Williams set the trend with a good point from play. Inspirational Tipperary corner-back, Liam Cronin, continued to dominate the game and, as Waterford began to wilt, Mark Sheahan and Brian Burke sent over a point each to level the game.

The next score was decisive! Cummins fielded a long free from Seán Maher and, from close-in, beat goalkeeper Kieran Cotter to put Tipperary in front for the very first time.

Full forward Oliver Costello replied soon after with a point to record Waterford's only score of the second-half. Tipperary tacked on three more points courtesy of Cummins, John Owens and substitute, Darren O'Connor, to take the honours and set up that semi-final meeting with Munster kingpins Kerry.

SCORERS - TIPPERARY: Brendan Cummins 1-2; Derry Foley 1-0; Mark Sheahan 0-1; Brian Burke 0-1; John Owens 0-1; James Williams 0-1; Darren O'Connor 0-1
WATERFORD: Gavin Keane 1-3; Shane Bergin 0-1; Oliver Costello 0-1

TIPPERARY

Martin Quinlivan

Conor O'Dwyer — Niall Kelly — Liam Cronin

Sean Collum — Brian Lacey — Bernard Hahessy

Derry Foley — Seán Maher

Mark Sheahan — John Owens — Brian Burke

James Williams — Dessie Lyons — Brendan Cummins

SUBSTITUTES: Christoir McGrath for James Williams; Darren O'Connor for Des Lyons

WATERFORD

Kieran Cotter

Niall Geary — Darrell Donnelly — Michael Fenton

Vinnie Murray — George Walsh — Liam Dalton

Don McMahon — Richie Power

David Whelan — Gavin Keane — Mark Radley

Stephen Cunningham — Oliver Costello — Shane Bergin

SUBSTITUTES: Tomas Gough for Stephen Cunningham;
Michael O'Brien for Mark Radley; William Kavanagh for David Whelan

TIPPERARY
BACK ROW L TO R: Brian Burke, Brian Lacey, Brendan Cummins, Derry Foley, Seán Maher, Niall Kelly, Bernard Hahessy, Mark Sheahan;
FRONT ROW L TO R: James Williams, Liam Cronin, Dessie Lyons, Martin Quinlivan, John Owens, Seán Collum, Conor O'Dwyer.

WATERFORD
BACK ROW L TO R: Richie Power, Don McMahon, Liam Dalton, Gavin Keane, George Walsh, Darrell Donnelly, Michael Fenton, Mark Radley;
FRONT ROW L TO R: Niall Geary, Oliver Costello, Vinnie Murray, Kieran Cotter, David Whelan, Stephen Cunningham, Shane Bergin.

SUNDAY, JUNE 22, 1997

MUNSTER SENIOR FOOTBALL CHAMPIONSHIP SEMI-FINAL

CLARE versus CORK

CUSACK PARK, ENNIS

REFEREE: MICHAEL CURLEY (GALWAY)

RESULT: CLARE 1-14 CORK 1-13

MARTIN DALY SCORED a sensational injury-time goal to give Clare footballers their first Championship victory over Cork in fifty-six years. Daly's last-ditch winner sparked off massive celebrations among Clare supporters in Cusack Park as shell-shocked Cork players slumped to the ground in utter disbelief.

Clare were somewhat unlucky not to beat Cork in last year's Championship after a replay, but the Banner men made amends in fairytale fashion. Cork were the architects of their own downfall through deplorable marksmanship, but credit brave Clare for a come-back of Lazarus-like porportions.

When midfielder Fachtna Collins restored Cork's three points advantage in the closing minute, it looked like Clare's brave fightback was all in vain. But the drama was only beginning! Daly converted a difficult free to reduce the margin to just two points. No one was quite prepared for what was about to unfold. A Cork attack came to nothing and then the drama began in earnest when Clare were awarded a free after Padraic Gallagher was fouled. Manager John O'Keeffe indicated to Ger Keane that a goal and nothing less would suffice. The quick-thinking Keane passed to Daly and somehow the Lissycasey marksman manage to evade two defenders before crashing a powerful shot to the net past a disbelieving Cork goalkeeper, Kevin Dwyer. A wonder goal that sent Clare supporters into ecstasy and stunned Cork followers into silence.

Cork players found it hard to comprehend that their Championship excursion was over for another twelve months. It was a game Cork should have won but, for their never-say-die attitude in the face of overwhelming odds, Clare deserved their victory. The Banner men had their backs to the wall for long periods of the second-half but Cork failed to press home their advantage and paid a heavy price for some appalling misses.

Clare started at a brisk pace and scored the opening three points before Cork took control through impressive work from midfielders, Pat Hegarty and Fachtna Collins. Brian Corcoran was dominant at centre-half-back while Colin Corkery and Joe Kavanagh were proving a handful for an overstretched Clare defence. Cork had edged one point in front when Stephen O'Brien rounded off a splendid movement involving Ciaran O'Sullivan and Martin Cronin by crashing the ball to the net.

Cork were ahead 1-9 to 0-7 at the half-time interval and Aidan Dorgan stretched their lead with a point immediately after the re-start. Cork then began to embark on a mission of self-destruction and kicked numerous wides to allow Clare back into the game. Francis McInerney's move to midfield was by now paying rich dividends and the Clare forwards began to prosper. Ger Keane scored a point from a free and substitute Cathal Shannon added another from play as Clare began the fightback in earnest. Keane scored three more points to reduce the margin to the very minimum by the 54th minute. Corkery and Collins steadied Cork nerves with a point apiece, but super-fit Clare continued to apply the pressure. Barry Keating and Collins exchanged points before Daly made an indelible imprint on the game and gave Clare their first Championship victory over Cork since 1941.

CLARE - SCORERS: Ger Keane 0 8; Martin Daly 1-3; Barry Keating 0-1; Michael Hynes 0-1; Cathal Shannon 0-1
CORK: Colin Corkery 0-4; Joe Kavanagh 0-3; Fachtna Collins 0-3; Stephen O'Brien 1-0; Brian Murphy 0-1; Aidan Dorgan 0-1; Brian Corcoran 0-1

CLARE

James Hanrahan

Alan Malone — Frankie Griffin — Padraig Gallagher

Barry Keating — Brendan Rouine — Aodáin Mac Cárthaigh

Donal O'Sullivan — Peter Cosgrove

Ger Keane — Francis McInerney — Michael Hynes

Padraig Conway — Odran O'Dwyer — Martin Daly

SUBSTITUTES: John Enright for Aodáin Mac Cárthaigh; Cathal Shannon for Padraig Conway; David Keane for Donal O'Sullivan

CORK

Kevin O'Dwyer

Brian Murphy — Mark O'Connor — Eoin Sexton

Ciaran O'Sullivan — Brian Corcoran — Podsie O'Mahony

Pat Hegarty — Fachtna Collins

Joe Kavanagh — Stephen O'Brien — Martin Cronin

Colin Corkery — John O'Driscoll — Aidan Dorgan

SUBSTITUTES: Mark O'Sullivan for Podsie O'Mahony; Ronan McCarthy for Martin Cronin; John Buckley for Aidan Dorgan

CLARE
BACK ROW L TO R: Odran O'Dwyer, Ger Keane, Francis McInerney, Donal O'Sullivan, Peter Cosgrove, Michael Hynes, Brendan Rouine, Martin Daly;
FRONT ROW L TO R: Alan Malone, Aodain Mac Cárthaigh, James Hanrahan, Padraig Conway, Barry Keating, Frankie Griffin, Padraig Gallagher.

CORK
BACK ROW L TO R: Brian Corcoran, Podsie O'Mahony, Joe Kavanagh, Colin Corkery, Pat Hegarty, Fachtna Collins, John O'Driscoll, Mark O'Connor;
FRONT ROW L TO R: Stephen O'Brien, Aidan Dorgan, Martin Cronin, Kevin O'Dwyer, Brian Murphy, Eoin Sexton, Ciaran O'Sullivan.

SUNDAY, JUNE 29, 1997

MUNSTER SENIOR FOOTBALL CHAMPIONSHIP SEMI-FINAL

KERRY versus TIPPERARY

AUSTIN STACK PARK, TRALEE

REFEREE: KEVIN WALSH (CLARE)

RESULT: KERRY 2-12 TIPPERARY 1-10

CLARE CREATED A MAJOR SHOCK when beating Cork the previous Sunday and an even bigger sensation looked to be on the cards until late in this game. League Champions Kerry eventually overcame the stubborn challenge of rank outsiders Tipperary to progress to a Munster Final meeting with Clare.

Kerry only led by a single point with less than ten minutes remaining but a splendid goal from Denis O'Dwyer turned the tide in favour of the defending champions. Before that crucial goal, Tipperary were performing like winners and had scored five points without reply to reduce the margin to the very minimum. Kerry manager Páidí Ó Sé had plenty of reason to be concerned until O'Dwyer scored the goal that effectively paved the way for a lack-lustre victory.

Kerry, making their first entry into Championship '97, were never more than moderate, but their persistence finally paid off despite the failure of the forward line to convert the many chances that came their way. Kerry shot ten wides in the first-half and that malaise continued to affect them throughout the game.

Kerry raced into a five points lead after 14 minutes but only scored twice for the remainder of the half to establish a 0-7 to 0-3 interval lead. Both Liam Hassett and John Brennan missed two gilt-edged goal chances in the opening half to further frustrate the Kingdom supporters.

Maurice Fitzgerald stretched Kerry's lead early in the second-half with his third point of the game. Then substitute John Crowley, who had replaced Dara Ó Cinnéide after 27 minutes, scored Kerry's first goal to push the champions 1-8 to 0-3 ahead. Tipperary goalkeeper Martin Quinlivan did exceptionally well to block a low-shot from Maurice Fitzgerald but Crowley struck the rebound to the net. Tipperary responded immediately with a magnificent goal from Declan Browne which gave fresh impetus to the team. The introduction of substitute Brendan Cummins had a significant bearing on the fightback and the Ardfinnan dual-star scored three points from frees as a resilient Tipperary side closed the gap to just one point. Kerry appeared vulnerable until O'Dwyer saw fit to put the supporters out of their misery with the clinching goal.

KERRY - SCORERS: Maurice Fitzgerald 0-7; John Crowley 1-1; Denis O'Dwyer 1-0; Liam Hassett 0-2; Dara Ó Sé 0-1; Killian Burns 0-1

TIPPERARY: Declan Browne 1-1; Brendan Cummins 0-3; Derry Foley 0-2; Seán Maher 0-1; Mark Sheahan 0-1; Brian Burke 0-1; Des Lyons 0-1

KERRY

Declan O'Keeffe

Seamus Moynihan | Barry O'Shea | Morgan O'Shea

Killian Burns | Liam O'Flaherty | Eamonn Breen

Dara Ó Sé | William Kirby

Pa Laide | Liam Hassett | Denis O'Dwyer

John Brennan | Dara Ó Cinnéide | Maurice Fitzgerald

SUBSTITUTES: John Crowley for Dara Ó Cinnéide; Michael Frances Russell for John Brennan; Donal Daly for William Kirby

TIPPERARY

Martin Quinlivan

Conor O'Dwyer | Niall Kelly | Liam Cronin

Brian Lacey | Sean Collum | Bernard Hahessy

Sean Maher | Derry Foley

Mark Sheahan | John Owens | Brian Burke

Dessie Lyons | Christóir McGrath | Declan Browne

SUBSTITUTES: Brendan Cummins for Bernard Hahessy; James Williams for Mark Sheahan

KERRY

BACK ROW L TO R: Dara Ó Sé, Barry O'Shea, Maurice Fitzgerald, Liam Hassett, Morgan O'Shea, Liam O'Flaherty, John Brennan; FRONT ROW L TO R: Pa Laide, Seamus Moynihan, Declan O'Keeffe, Dara Ó Cinnéide, Denis O'Dwyer, William Kirby, Killian Burns, Eamonn Breen.

TIPPERARY
BACK ROW L TO R: Niall Kelly, Christóir McGrath, Brian Burke, Seán Maher, Derry Foley, Brian Lacey, Dessie Lyons, Mark Sheahan;
FRONT ROW L TO R: Bernard Hahessy, Conor O'Dwyer, Seán Collum, Martin Quinlivan, Declan Browne, Liam Cronin, John Owens.

SUNDAY, JULY 20, 1997

MUNSTER SENIOR FOOTBALL CHAMPIONSHIP FINAL

KERRY versus CLARE

GAELIC GROUNDS, LIMERICK

REFEREE: NIALL BARRETT

RESULT: KERRY 1-13 CLARE 0-11

GOALSCORING HERO, Pa Laide, emerged as 'Man of the Match' as Kerry successfully defended their Munster crown by virtue of a five points victory over Clare at the Gaelic Grounds. Austin Stack's player, Laide, somehow got hold of a high ball from centre-half-back, Liam O'Flaherty, no more than three minutes after the re-start, and sprinted clear before unleashing a powerful shot for a wonder goal. Laide's superb goal was the highlight of a game that Kerry always looked likely to win, but which still hung in the balance right up until the final five minutes when the contribution of substitutes, Michael Francis Russell and John Crowley, proved decisive.

Kerry were never behind in a game where their forwards combined well as a unit and produced some excellent scores, in particular from lightning-fast Laide, All-Star Maurice Fitzgerald and Dara Ó Cinnéide. The Kerry defence performed admirably and, as manager Páidí Ó Sé stated afterwards, "We didn't give Clare one clear chance of a goal out there today. We learned a lot from watching Clare's victory over Cork and our defence coped very well."

The in-form Martin Daly was a constant threat to the Kerry rearguard and his fifth point of the game after 59 minutes brought Clare to within two points of the champions. But with impressive substitutes Russell and Crowley rowing in with a point each and with Laide rounding off a magnificent individual display by scoring the final point of the afternoon, Kerry deservedly retained the Munster Championship with five points to spare.

Kerry took a grip on the game very early on and had moved into a 0-5 to 0-2 lead by the 11th minute with Maurice Fitzgerald firing over two points and Denis O'Dwyer, Dara Ó Cinnéide and Brian Clarke landing one each. Fitzgerald was the dominant player in the early stages but a let-off for Clare when the brilliant St. Mary's man hit the side netting after just nine minutes play.

Donal O'Sullivan and Michael Hynes gave Clare a distinct advantage at midfield and two points from Daly and a point from substitute, Frank Lohan, on the half-hour reduced the margin to the minimum. Defenders Frankie Griffin and Barry Keating were playing confidently and Kerry were restricted to just three points in the closing eighteen minutes of the first-half.

Kerry held a three points advantage, 0-8 to 0-5, at the interval but Laide's magnificent goal after 38 minutes rocked Clare back on their heels. It was a huge setback for the Bannermen as they had completely dominated the opening three minutes of the second half but missed a number of good scoring chances. However, Kerry were unable to capitalise on Laide's 'golden goal' and instead Clare hit back in determined fashion with four points without reply to put a less-than-confident Kerry on the ropes. During that period of Clare dominance, their goalkeeper, James Hanrahan, brought off a great save to deprive Maurice Fitzgerald a certain goal.

The game was still on a knife-edge entering the final stages with Kerry doggedly holding on to a slender two points lead, but Clare paid a heavy price for missing a few scoring opportunities at a crucial stage. Russell and Crowley steadied Kerry nerves with a point apiece and Laide capped a magnificent display with the final point of the game.

SCORERS - KERRY: Maurice Fitzgerald 0-5; Pa Laide 1-2; Dara Ó Cinnéide 0-2; Michael Francis Russell 0-1; Denis O'Dwyer 0-1; Brian Clarke 0-1; John Crowley 0-1
CLARE: Martin Daly 0-5; Ger Keane 0-4; John Enright 0-1; Frank Lohan 0-1

KERRY

Declan O'Keeffe

Mike Hassett — Barry O'Shea — Killian Burns

Seamus Moynihan — Liam O'Flaherty — Eamonn Breen

William Kirby — Dara Ó Sé

Pa Laide — Liam Hassett — Denis O'Dwyer

Dara Ó Cinnéide — Brian Clarke — Maurice Fitzgerald

SUBSTITUTES: Michael Francis Russell for Brian Clarke; John Crowley for Denis O'Dwyer; Billy O'Shea for Mike Hassett

CLARE

James Hanrahan

Padraig Gallagher | Frankie Griffin | Alan Malone

Barry Keating | Brendan Rouine | John Enright

Donal O'Sullivan | Michael Hynes

Ger Keane | Francis McInerney | Cathal Shannon

Odran O'Dwyer | David Keane | Martin Daly

SUBSTITUTES: Frank Lohan for David Keane; Padraig Conway for Cathal Shannon; Aidan O'Keeffe for Frank Lohan

KERRY
BACK ROW L TO R: Dara Ó Sé, Barry O'Shea, Liam O'Flaherty; Liam Hassett; Seamus Moynihan, Maurice Fitzgerald, Brian Clarke;
FRONT ROW L TO R: Pa Laide, William Kirby, Declan O'Keeffe, Mike Hassett, Killian Burns, Dara Ó Cinnéide, Denis O'Dwyer, Eamonn Breen.

CLARE
BACK ROW L TO R: Odran O'Dwyer, Cathal Shannon, Donal O'Sullivan, Francis McInerney, Michael Hynes, James Hanrahan, Martin Daly, Brendan Rouine;
FRONT ROW L TO R: David Keane, John Enright, Frankie Griffin, Padraig Gallagher, Barry Keating, Alan Malone, Ger Keane.

SUNDAY, MAY 25, 1997

CONNACHT SENIOR FOOTBALL CHAMPIONSHIP FIRST ROUND

MAYO versus GALWAY

TUAM STADIUM

REFEREE: EDDIE NEARY (SLIGO)

RESULT: MAYO 1-16 GALWAY 0-15

PROUD MAYO ONCE AGAIN proved the doubters wrong! There were real fears even among some of their most ardent supporters that last year's defeat by Meath in the All-Ireland final replay may have caused irreparable damage to morale among the players. But supporters can have all the doubts in the world provided the malaise is not allowed to permeate through the team and there was never any real danger that manager John Maughan would let that happen. The Mayo team had worked hard to put behind them the disappointment of losing the All-Ireland final replay in such dramatic circumstances for what was an acid test against their arch-rivals Galway.

Mayo had failed to beat Galway in a Championship game at Tuam Stadium since 1951 and the presence at the game of U.S. based Dr. Padraic Carney, who played on that last victorious team 46 years before, underlined the significance of the occasion on what was a momentous event in the North Galway town.

It was billed as the game of the day and it certainly lived up to expectations. I was commentating on the game for RTE Radio Sport and found it to be one of the most thoroughly enjoyable and intensely exciting games of the entire Championship. Players from both sides ran themselves to a standstill in pursuit of glory on what was a boiling hot day. There were some text-book scores from both play and frees; wonderful passing movements and some individual performances that marked this game as something very special.

The stakes were high and the tension was palpable. Mayo full-forward John Casey was stretched on the ground just before the throw-in after an altercation with Galway full-back, Gary Fahy. Sligo referee Eddie Neary booked both players before proceeding to get the game underway.

Mayo dictated the early exchanges and their goal from P.J. Loftus after little more than two minutes play followed good work by David Nestor, Liam McHale and John Casey. It was a short kick-out by Galway goalkeeper Martin McNamara which ultimately led to the goal after Gary Fahy was caught in possession. Indeed, the short kick-out strategy adopted by Galway proved their undoing in the closing stages of the game and allowed Mayo through for vital scores.

Mayo led by 1-4 to no score after nine minutes and at that stage there was little to suggest Galway could claw their way back into contention. Seán ÓDomhnaill, John Donnellan and Niall Finnegan were prominent in Galway's revival. The margin was down to a more manageable five points after 22 minutes as Galway began to find chinks in the Mayo defence.

Galway scored nine points to Mayo's miserly total of two in the closing twenty-three minutes of the first-half. Michael Donnellan's switch to centre-half-forward had a huge bearing on the turnaround. Player manager, Val Daly, had struggled against James Nallen, but Donnellan fared much better against the brilliant Crossmolina man and came close to scoring a spectacular goal when the ball went narrowly wide. That near miss, and some excellent points from Niall Finnegan, John Donnellan, Declan Meehan and Val Daly, clearly indicated that the pendulum had swung in favour of Galway as the first-half came to a close with the sides level, 1-6 to 0-9. That dramatic fade-out was a cause for concern for Mayo and there was more cause for worry when John Donnellan edged Galway in front for the very first time shortly after the re-start. Soon afterwards Finnegan stretched Galway's lead with his sixth point of the game.

John Casey sent over a fine point to record Mayo's first score for all of thirty-four minutes. Slowly but surely, Mayo regained the initiative and were looking more assured and confident by the time Maurice Sheridan landed a wonderful long-range point to put his side back in front after 49 minutes. All-Star Pat Holmes had by then replaced Dermot Flanagan and was playing confidently, while another substitute, Kieran McDonald, was making his presence felt and he chipped in with two points from play. Galway faded in the closing quarter but Finnegan kept them in touch with some good points. Although Finnegan missed a close-in free at a crucial stage, the Salthill clubman had an outstanding game and accounted for nine points in a polished display. Maurice Sheridan scored eight points to once again illustrate his importance to this Mayo team - a team that appears to have fully recovered from the hangover of last year's All-Ireland Final defeat.

SCORERS - MAYO: Maurice Sheridan 0-8; P.J. Loftus 1-0; David Nestor 0-2; Liam McHale 0-2; Kieran McDonald 0-2; John Casey 0-1; Pat Fallon 0-1
GALWAY: Niall Finnegan 0-9; John Donnellan 0-3; Declan Meehan 0-1; Val Daly 0-1; Seán Óg De Paor 0-1;

MAYO

Peter Burke

Dermot Flanagan — Kevin Cahill — Kenneth Mortimer

Fergal Costello — James Nallen — Noel Connelly

Colm McManamon — Pat Fallon

Maurice Sheridan — Liam McHale — James Horan

David Nestor — John Casey — P.J. Loftus

SUBSTITUTES: Kieran McDonald for James Horan; Pat Holmes for Dermot Flanagan; Ronan Golding for P.J. Loftus

GALWAY

Martin McNamara

Francis McWalter — Gary Fahy — Thomas Meehan

Seán Óg de Paor — Ray Silke — Tomás Mannion

Damien Mitchell — Sean Ó Domhnaill

Declan Meehan — Val Daly — Michael Donnellan

Tommy Carton — Niall Finnegan — John Donnellan

SUBSTITUTES: Fergal O'Neill for Declan Meehan; Alan Mulholland for Val Daly; Tommie Wilson for Tommy Carton

MAYO

BACK ROW L TO R: Liam McHale, James Horan, Pat Fallon, John Casey, Peter Burke, James Nallen, Maurice Sheridan, Kevin Cahill; FRONT ROW: P.J. Loftus, Fergal Costello, Kenneth Mortimer, Noel Connelly, Colm McManamon, Dermot Flanagan, David Nestor.

GALWAY

BACK ROW L TO R: Val Daly, Seán Ó Domhnaill, Gary Fahy, John Donnellan, Francis McWalter, Thomas Meehan, Tomás Mannion; FRONT ROW L TO R: Ray Silke, Niall Finnegan, Martin McNamara, Seán Óg de Paor, Michael Donnellan, Tommy Carton, Declan Meehan, Damien Mitchell.

SUNDAY, JUNE 1, 1997

CONNACHT SENIOR FOOTBALL CHAMPIONSHIP FIRST ROUND

LEITRIM versus LONDON

RUISLIP PARK, LONDON

REFEREE: DES JOYCE (GALWAY)

RESULT: LEITRIM 2-18 LONDON 1-13 (AFTER EXTRA TIME)

IN LAST YEAR'S Championship Book, my opening paragraph on the report of the Mayo/London game read thus: "It appears a trip to play London in the Connacht Championship can no longer be considered just a relaxing weekend for the visiting team rounded off with the customary drubbing of the Exiles at Ruislip Park." The exact same sentiments apply this year!

If Mayo were given a stern test last year before eventually winning by six points, then Leitrim got the fright of their lives before their inspirational captain, Declan Darcy, converted a last-minute penalty to force a draw. Leitrim won comfortably by eight points in extra-time to advance to a Connacht semi-final meeting with holders Mayo at McHale Park.

Rank outsiders London looked set for a shock victory when substitute Frank Hussey scored a goal little more than three minutes before the finish to edge his side ahead by three points on a 1-9 to 0-9 scoreline. Leitrim goalkeeper, Martin McHugh, appeared to misjudge the flight of the ball and Hussey crashed the ball to the net. But just when it appeared Leitrim were about to exit Championship '97, referee Des Joyce awarded the visitors a controversial penalty, much to the dismay of the large home following. The referee adjudged that Leitrim forward Adrian Cullen had been fouled and had no hesitation in awarding the penalty.

London players vehemently protested against the decision but their pleas fell on deaf ears and their chance of a sensational victory disappeared when Dublin-born Darcy converted the penalty in confident fashion.

Favoured by a stiff breeze, London dominated the opening half and had forged ahead, 0-6 to 0-1, at the interval. Mick Hesnan and Senan Hehir dominated proceedings at midfield as the windy conditions caused problems for both sets of players. Tommy Maguire was prominent in the London attack and kicked the opening two points while promising teenager Paul Hehir extended the Exiles' lead with a point from a '45. It took Leitrim some 21 minutes to record their only score of the first half, a point from corner-forward, Fintan McBrien.

London finished the first-half on a high note when Mick Hesnan, Senan Hehir and Aidan Creamer combined to send Stevie Kane through for an excellent point.

London extended their lead early in the second-half with a point each from Tommy Maguire and Paul Hehir as Leitrim struggled to make any impression. However, Darcy soon began to exert his influence on the game and his many fine scores brought Leitrim back into contention. Darcy was the outstanding player on view and were it not for his immense contribution, the 1994 Connacht Champions would have suffered a humiliating defeat. Veteran Mickey Quinn, Leitrim's first ever All-Star, also had a huge influence on the game when introduced in place of Jason Ward after 49 minutes play.

Leitrim's superior fitness had a significant bearing in the extra-time period and the result was never in doubt once Darcy scored his second goal. The Leitrim captain was truly magnificent all through and his tally of 2-10 represented the highest individual score of Championship '97'.

SCORERS - LEITRIM: Declan Darcy 2-10; Fintan McBrien 0-4; Jimmy Guckian 0-1; Padraig McLoughlin 0-1; Gerry Flanagan 0-1; George Dugdale 0-1;
LONDON: Tommy Maguire 0-5; Paul Hehir 0-4; Frank Hussey 1-0; Senan Hehir 0-2; Stevie Kane 0-1; Darren Gaffney 0-1

LEITRIM

Martin McHugh

Joe Honeyman — Seamus Quinn — Fergal Reynolds

Noel Moran — Killian McLoughlin — Ciaran Murray

Jason Ward — Benny Guckian

George Dugdale — Declan Darcy — Jimmy Guckian

Adrian Cullen — Adrian Charle — Fintan McBrien

SUBSTITUTES: Padraig McLoughlin for Adrian Charles; Mickey Quinn for Jason Ward; Gerry Flanagan for Joe Honeyman
(EXTRA-TIME) Joe Tiffoney for Fergal Reynolds

LONDON

John Collins

Stevie Kane — Diarmuid Gordon — Mark Smith

Pascal Cullen — Barry McDonagh — Ciaran Byrne

Mick Hesnan — Senan Hehir

Paul Hehir — Timmy Connolly — Aiden Creamer

Paul Coggins — Darren Gaffey — Tommy Maguire

SUBSTITUTES: Frank Hussey for Aiden Creamer;
Robert Walsh for Mark Smith; Tony Murphy for Mick Hesnan

LEITRIM
BACK ROW L TO R: Jimmy Guckian, Adrian Cullen, Benny Guckian, Martin McHugh, Ciaran Murray, Adrian Charles, Seamus Quinn, George Dugdale;
FRONT ROW L TO R: Fergal Reynolds, Killian McLoughlin, Declan Darcy, Jason Ward, Fintan McBrien, Joe Honeyman, Noel Moran.

SUNDAY, JUNE 22, 1997

CONNACHT SENIOR FOOTBALL CHAMPIONSHIP SEMI-FINAL

SLIGO versus ROSCOMMON

MARKIEVICZ PARK, SLIGO

REFEREE: SEAMUS PRIOR (LEITRIM)

RESULT: SLIGO 1-14 ROSCOMMON 1-11

SLIGO FOOTBALLERS have had precious little to celebrate in recent years, but their win against favourites Roscommon provided a welcome respite for their success-starved supporters. Sligo thoroughly deserved their victory against a Roscommon team that hit a succession of wides in the second-half and ultimately paid a heavy price for their wastefulness. Roscommon were strongly fancied to advance to the Connacht Final, but Sligo manager Mickey Moran had his homework done and his highly motivated team overcame the odds to win with three points to spare.

Perhaps the signs were ominous! Sligo drew with Galway in both the '95 and '96 Championships and even though they had little joy in the replays, the seeds had been sown. Former Derry manager Moran reshaped the team and the younger players responded to the challenge with a confidence that belied their tender years. There were seven players that featured in last year's replay against Galway in action against Roscommon and their experience proved very valuable in times of crisis.

Interestingly, Paul Taylor scored an aggregate total of 1-10 in the two games against Galway last year, and the same player made an indelible imprint in the game against Roscommon with the very considerable tally of nine points. His contribution from play and frees ensured a rare Championship victory for his county.

Despite playing against a stiff breeze, Sligo began in confident fashion and had three points on the scoreboard before sluggish Roscommon got off the mark with a point from Luke Dolan after 12 minutes. Gradually Roscommon took complete control and in a fifteen-minute purple patch, scored a further eight points without reply. Roscommon played some outstanding football during that period of dominance with Nigel Dineen, Luke Dolan, Tom Ryan, Don Connellan and Alan Nolan kicking over some excellent points from play.

Roscommon's best chance of a goal in the first-half fell to their corner-forward, Niall O'Donoghue, after he got on the end of a high ball from the right wing from Don Connellan. O'Donoghue rounded the advancing Sligo goalkeeper, Pat Kilcoyne, but his goalbound shot was bravely deflected over the crossbar by corner-back, Neil Carew.

Still, Roscommon led by double scores, 0-10 to 0-5, at half-time but within four minutes of the re-start the margin had been reduced to three points courtesy of a point each from Eamon O'Hara and the impressive Taylor.

Then came a stage when absolutely nothing went right for Roscommon and they missed numerous opportunities from eminently scoreable positions. Their ever-loyal supporters looked on in utter disbelief as one chance after another was spurned with disastrous consequences.

Sligo took full advantage of Roscommon's dreadful marksmanship and Taylor, Philip Neary and Dessie Sloyan showed the visitors how it should be done with some well taken points.

To compound Roscommon's misfortune, Sligo scored a somewhat fortuitous goal which effectively clinched the issue. Roscommon goalkeeper Shane Curran lost possession, did well to recover, only to deliver a short pass to the unsuspecting Martin Feely. The full-back was dispossessed by Dessie Sloyane and Philip Neary struck a ground shot to the net for a golden goal.

Neary and Taylor stretched Sligo's advantage with a point each before Tom Ryan with a point from play registered Roscommon's first score for over thirty minutes.

The impressive Ryan scored a goal near the finish as Roscommon fought tooth-and-nail to rescue the game.

Corner-forward Nigel Dineen's initial effort was blocked by goalkeeper, Pat Kilcoyne, but Ryan was on hand to first-time the ball to the net.

SCORERS - SLIGO: Paul Taylor 0-9; Philip Neary 1-3; Eamonn O'Hara 0-1; Dessie Sloyane 0-1
ROSCOMMON: Tom Ryan 1-2; Luke Dolan 0-4; Nigel Dineen 0-2; Don Connellan 0-1;
Alan Nolan 0-1; Niall O'Donoghue 0-1

SLIGO

	Pat Kilcoyne	
Mark Cosgrove	Colin White	Neil Carew
Bernard Mulhern	Nigel Clancy	Brendan Kilcoyne
Paul Durcan		Dermot Kevany
Ken Killeen	Eamonn O'Hara	Philip Neary
Dessie Sloyane	Paul Taylor	Gerry McGowan

SUBSTITUTES: Brian Walsh for Ken Killeen; Paul Seevers for Dermot Kevany

ROSCOMMON

	Shane Curran	
Sean Staunton	Martin Feely	Enon Gavin
Rossa O'Callaghan	Clifford McDonald	Ciaran Heneghan
Tom Ryan		Derek Duggan
Luke Dolan	Alan Nolan	David O'Connor
Nigel Dineen	Don Connellan	Niall O'Donoghue

SUBSTITUTES: Damien Donlon for David O'Connor;
Tom Lennon for Derek Duggan

SUNDAY, JUNE 29, 1997

CONNACHT SENIOR FOOTBALL CHAMPIONSHIP SEMI-FINAL

MAYO versus LEITRIM

McHALE PARK, CASTLEBAR

REFEREE: MICHAEL CURLEY (GALWAY)

RESULT: MAYO 0-18 LEITRIM 0-11

MAYO MARCHED on to a Connacht Final meeting with Sligo by disposing of the Leitrim challenge with an authoritative and decisive display before an attendance of over 23,000 at McHale Park.

But there was a very definite downside to Mayo's victory! An ugly fracas near the finish, involving a number of players from both sides, resulted in Mayo's Colm McManamon and Leitrim's Gerry Flanagan being ordered off by Galway referee, Michael Curley. McManamon, suspended for his part in the brawl which marred last year's All-Ireland final replay, received his marching orders for striking Leitrim defender Seamus Quinn in the face. McManamon's actions sparked off an ugly punch-up which involved a number of players and was totally out of context with the rest of the game. McManamon and Flanagan were the only players to be sent off as several others became embroiled in the fracas. McManamon left the field with blood streaming from a nasty looking eye injury while Mayo manager, John Maughan, was knocked to the ground by a punch to the face.

The unwanted punch-up was the main talking point at the finish of what otherwise was a sporting, if at times, over-physical game.

Mayo were dealt a blow before the start when star corner-forward, David Nestor, was ruled out because of injury. All-Star Pat Holmes was drafted in at centre-half-back as manager Maughan made wholesale positional switches. James Nallen was moved to mid-field with basketball international Liam McHale being switched to centre-half-forward. Colm McManamon started at left-half-forward and Maurice Sheridan played at right-half-forward with James Horan at left corner forward in place of Nestor.

Leitrim began in confident fashion and led by 0-2 to 0-1 early on as Mayo struggled to find their rhythm and squandered several scoring opportunities. Maurice Sheridan sent over the equalising point after twenty minutes and soon after, the impressive Kieran McDonald landed the lead point. The champions found scores hard to come by in the opening quarter, but enjoyed much more success in the closing stages of the half with Sheridan, Liam McHale, James Horan, McDonald and John Casey all on target. Mayo full-back Kevin Cahill had to retire injured after 29 minutes and was replaced by Diarmuid Byrne, as army-man Maughan reshuffled his forces once again. The half ended with Mayo leading by six points, 0-8 to 0-2.

Substitute Byrne got his name on the scoresheet with the opening point of the sec-ond-half and further Mayo points from speedy corner-back, Kenneth Mortimer, and free-taker Maurice Sheridan pushed the defending champions eight points clear. Leitrim were winning a lot of possession at midfield but were unable to make inroads against a water-tight Mayo defence in which Mortimer, Holmes and Nallen, in particular, were very prominent. Nallen proved once again that he is one of the finest defenders in present day gaelic football.

Inspirational Leitrim captain, Declan Darcy, scorer of 2-10 against London in the previous round, continued to work hard against the odds and scored a fine point after 43 minutes. It was Leitrim's first score for more than twenty-nine minutes. That statistic alone underlines Leitrim's dearth of scoring forwards and illustrates Mayo's defensive strengths. Darcy, Mickey Quinn, Killian McLoughlin and Seamus Quinn worked tireless-ly for Leitrim in a vain attempt to turn the tide. Darcy emerged as top scorer with seven points while Mickey Quinn, Leitrim's first-ever All-Star, gave yet another tour-de-force display in what was his twentieth year playing senior Championship football.

Leitrim full-forward Adrian Cullen had the best chance of a goal when he caught a long ball from Noel Moran inside the Mayo defence 15 minutes into the second-half, but his powerful shot sailed over the crossbar

Maurice Sheridan punished indiscretions by the Leitrim defence and ended the day with a tally of six points from frees - four in the second half. Pat Fallon turned in one of his best ever performances for the county, while young Crossmolina player, Kieran McDonald, has developed into a forward of real class. His four points from play were all expertly taken.

Leitrim finished strongly with the last three points of the game, but by that stage, Mayo had their work done and had booked their passage to a Connacht final meeting with surprise packets Sligo.

SCORERS - MAYO: Maurice Sheridan 0-6; Kieran McDonald 0-4; Diarmuid Byrne 0-2; Kenneth Mortimer 0-1; Liam McHale 0-1; James Horan 0-1; James Nallen 0-1; John Casey 0-1; P.J. Loftus 0-1
LEITRIM: Declan Darcy 0-7; Adrian Cullen 0-2; Fintan McBrien 0-1; Padraig McLoughlin 0-1

MAYO

Peter Burke

Kenneth Mortimer — Kevin Cahill — Dermot Flanagan

Fergal Costello — Pat Holmes — Noel Connelly

James Nallen — Pat Fallon

Maurice Sheridan — Liam McHale — Colm McManamon

Kieran McDonald — John Casey — James Horan

SUBSTITUTES: Diarmuid Byrne for Kevin Cahill;
P.J. Loftus for James Horan; David Heaney for Liam McHale

LEITRIM

Martin McHugh

Joe Honeyman — Seamus Quinn — Ciaran Murray

Noel Moran — Killian McLoughlin — Gerry Flanagan

Mickey Quinn — Benny Guckian

George Dugdale — Declan Darcy — Jason Ward

Adrian Cullen — Adrian Charles — Fintan McBrien

SUBSTITUTES: Padraig McLoughlin for Jason Ward;
Aidan Rooney for Adrian Charles; Pat Donoghue for Brendan Guckian

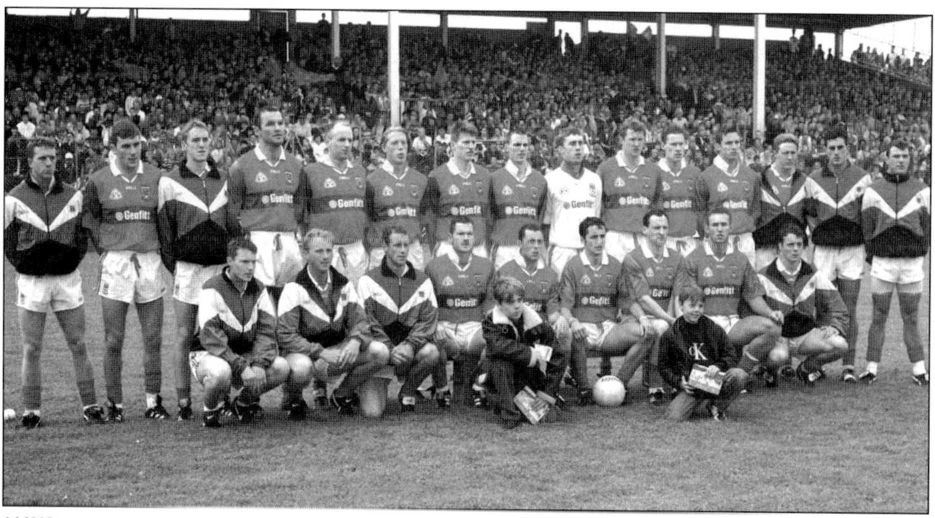

MAYO
BACK ROW L TO R: Brian Heffernan, James Horan, David Heaney, Liam McHale, Pat Holmes, Kieran McDonald, Kevin Cahill, John Casey, Peter Burke, Pat Fallon, James Nallen, Maurice Sheridan, Ronan Goulding, John Madden, P.J. Loftus;
FRONT ROW L TO R: Diarmuid Byrne, Tony Morley, Michael Gardiner, Fergal Costello, Kenneth Mortimer, Noel Connelly, Dermot Flanagan, Colm McManamon, Ray Connelly.

LEITRIM
BACK ROW L TO R: Seamus Quinn, Adrian Cullen, Adrian Charles, Martin McHugh, Jason Ward, George Dugdale, Mickey Quinn, Noel Moran;
FRONT ROW L TO R: Ciaran Murray, Gerry Flanagan, Killian McLoughlin, Declan Darcy, Benny Guckian, Fintan McBrien, Joe Honeyman;

SUNDAY, AUGUST 3, 1997

CONNACHT SENIOR FOOTBALL FINAL

MAYO versus SLIGO

DR. HYDE PARK, ROSCOMMON

REFEREE: MICHAEL CURLEY (GALWAY)

RESULT: MAYO 0-11 SLIGO 1-7

MAYO RETAINED their Connacht football title with a less than impressive performance against a Sligo team that defied the odds with a gutsy performance that tested the defending champions to the limit. It was poor quality fare throughout, and the game only came to life in the closing minutes when Sligo scored 1-2 without reply and threatened to spoil the Mayo party. However, referee Michael Curley blew the final whistle after little more than 20 seconds injury-time to deprive resurgent Sligo a chance to snatch an equalising point.

Manager John Maughan was none too pleased with Mayo's inept display which was lacking the passion and purpose so evident against Galway in the first round game in late May. Far too many Mayo players performed well below par and a repeat showing in the All-Ireland semi-final against the Leinster champions would surely mean further misery for this proud footballing county.

Sligo started in confident fashion, and a point each from Paul Taylor and Ken Killeen left them 0-2 to 0-1 ahead after 10 minutes play. However, with Liam McHale getting into his stride at midfield, and with forwards Kieran McDonald, Maurice Sheridan and David Nestor showing good early form, Mayo soon took control and had built up a 0-5 to 0-2 lead after 20 minutes. That fifth point for Mayo from Ronan Golding proved controversial and ultimately decisive. The umpires were clearly undecided but the white flag was eventually raised after consultation with the referee. Corner-forward McDonald scored Mayo's first two points but then inexplicably proceeded to hit a succession of wides. Sheridan scored an excellent long-range point from play in the closing stages of the first-half, but untypically also missed a few chances.

Sligo's solitary point in the closing twenty-five minutes of the opening half was scored by Dessie Sloyane and only the brilliance of goalkeeper Pat Kilcoyne kept the margin down to four points at the interval.

Kilcoyne brought off a superb save from John Casey early in the game and he deprived the Charlestown player another goal three minutes before the break. David Nestor also failed to beat the Sligo goalkeeper when the opportunity presented itself late in the opening half. Nestor was one of the few Mayo players to do himself justice in an eminently forgettable game. The vastly experienced Dermot Flanagan also turned in a fine display. His steadying influence under pressure was invaluable and he made a few timely interceptions to stave-off danger. He cleared off the line late in the first-half and also deprived Sligo a certain goal on another occasion. It was a fitting performance for a player winning his seventh Connacht Championship medal, the first Mayo player to achieve that feat. An outstanding ambassador! Pat Fallon was another Mayo player to enhance his reputation.

Mayo scored just four points in the entire second-half with Sheridan once again very much to the fore. His third pointed free of the second-half helped Mayo establish a comfortable 0-10 to 0-5 lead after 60 minutes. There was little urgency about Mayo's play, perhaps complacency was a factor. David Nestor scored his first point of the game with less than ten minutes remaining to give the champions an unassailable six points advantage.

Then, just as supporters began to stream out of Dr. Hyde Park, Sligo began their amazing comeback. Nestor had a great chance to finish Sligo off but shot wide; Paul Taylor incredibly missed a close-in free but made amends a short time later with a point from play. Sligo wing-forward, Brian Walsh, scored a late goal and Paul Durcan tacked on a point to ensure a grandstand finish. The match ended sooner than anticipated when referee Michael Curley blew the full-time whistle less than twenty seconds into injury-time. The dramatic finish disguised what otherwise was a mediocre Connacht Final that left Mayo with a lot of unanswered questions ahead of their second successive All-Ireland semi-final appearance.

SCORERS - MAYO: Maurice Sheridan 0-6; Ciaran McDonald 0-2; David Nestor 0-1; James Horan 0-1; Ronan Golding 0-1

SLIGO: Brian Walsh 1-1; Paul Taylor 0-2; Dessie Sloyane 0-1; Paul Durcan 0-1; Ken Killeen 0-1; Eamonn O'Hara 0-1

MAYO

	Peter Burke	
Kenneth Mortimer	Pat Holmes	Dermot Flanagan
Fergal Costello	James Nallen	Noel Connelly
Liam McHale		Pat Fallon
David Nestor	James Horan	Maurice Sheridan
Kieran McDonald	John Casey	Ronan Golding

SUBSTITUTES: Kevin O'Neill for Ronan Golding; Diarmuid Byrne for James Horan

SLIGO

	Pat Kilcoyne	
Mark Cosgrove	Colin White	Neil Carew
Bernard Mulhern	Nigel Clancy	Brendan Kilcoyne
Paul Durcan		Dermot Kevany
Ken Killeen	Eamonn O'Hara	Brian Walsh
Dessie Sloyane	Paul Taylor	Gerry McGowan

SUBSTITUTES: David Durkin for Bernard Mulhern;
Sean Davy for Dessie Sloyane; Eamonn Cawley for Dermot Kevany

MAYO
BACK ROW L TO R: Liam McHale, Pat Holmes, Ronan Golding, Kieran McDonald, John Casey, Peter Burke, Pat Fallon, Maurice Sheridan, James Nallen;
FRONT ROW L TO R: James Horan, Fergal Costello, Noel Connelly, Kenneth Mortimer, Dermot Flanagan, David Nestor.

SLIGO
BACK ROW L TO R: Colin White, Paul Durcan, Pat Kilcoyne, Nigel Clancy, Dermot Kevany, Mark Cosgrove, Brian Walsh, Eamonn O'Hara;
FRONT ROW L TO R: Paul Taylor, Bernard Mulhern, Brendan Kilcoyne, Gerry McGowan, Neil Carew, Ken Killeen, Dessie Sloyane.

SUNDAY, MAY 11, 1997

LEINSTER SENIOR FOOTBALL CHAMPIONSHIP PRELIMINARY ROUND

OFFALY versus LONGFORD

O'CONNOR PARK, TULLAMORE

REFEREE: ADRIAN WALSH, DUBLIN

RESULT: OFFALY 5-17 LONGFORD 0-13

DEVELOPMENTS ELSEWHERE in sport ensured there was a low-key build-up to the opening day of the 1997 All-Ireland Football Championship. The six counties entering the fray on Sunday, May 11, with the exception of Offaly, were all regarded as out-and-out no-hopers in their quest for either provincial or All-Ireland honours. Furthermore, sports reporters from radio, television and the print media had plenty to occupy their minds in the early part of the week to avoid getting unduly worked up about forthcoming events at Tullamore, New Ross and Limerick.

After all, Kerry footballers had defeated Cork at Páirc Uí Chaoimh to win their sixteenth National League title on Sunday, May 4, and the manner of their impressive victory was well documented in all sections of the media.

It was Kerry's first national senior football title since their 1986 All-Ireland victory over Tyrone.

Then Dubliner Ken Doherty's magnificent achievement in becoming the first player from the Republic Of Ireland to win the World Snooker Championship overshadowed all other sporting matters from Monday evening until Thursday. Manchester United also grabbed their share of the headlines that week after winning their fourth English Premiership title in five years.

By the weekend, however, managers and players from the six competing counties in the Championship were figuring much more prominently: defending team selections, assessing strengths and weaknesses, and, as usual, making predictions.

Offaly and Longford had the proud honour of ushering in the 1997 All-Ireland Senior Football Championship as their game in Tullamore began slightly earlier than the second Leinster Championship tie at New Ross between Wexford and Westmeath and the meeting of Limerick and Tipperary at the Gaelic Grounds. Among the interested spectators in Tullamore were Ard Stiurthoir, Chumann Luthcleas Gael, Liam Mulvihill, himself a native of Longford, and former President, Jack Boothman, wearing his trademark peak cap to stave off the wintry elements.

Offaly manager, Tommy Lyons, who guided Dublin side Kilmacud Crokes to a first All-Ireland Club title in 1995, was careful not to underestimate Longford in the build-up to the Championship opener in which his side were justifiable favourites. Offaly had an impressive unbeaten run in Division Four of the League and were somewhat unfortunate to lose by a single point to Division One pacesetters Kildare in the quarter-final of the competition. Conversely, Longford had a quite disastrous League campaign which resulted in their relegation from Division Three, much to the dismay of their supporters, who were also disappointed that their team lost following a replay to Fermanagh in the All-Ireland 'B' Final. That defeat by Fermanagh did untold damage to morale among the Longford players.

The fact that Laois agreed to an Offaly request to play their Division One hurling league game as a curtain- raiser to the Championship clash ensured a large turn-out for the double-header. Offaly defeated bottom of the table Laois by three points in a closely contested hurling game to put the home supporters in the right frame of mind as they awaited their county footballers' first foray into Championship '97.

Both Offaly and Longford had lost in the opening round twelve months previously, but a new Championship year always brings fresh hope among players and supporters alike. Offaly gave a vote of confidence to the team that lost to Kildare in the quarter-final, while Longford manager, Eamon Coleman, opted to give Championship debuts to no less than six players: goalkeeper Gavin Tonra along with defenders Cathal Conefry, Gary Brady, Enda Ledwith, Ollie Reilly and Ciaran Keogh.

During a brief visit to the Offaly and Longford dressingrooms before the game, I found both managers in a confident mood. Some Longford supporters I spoke with shortly before the game expressed the fear that the wet conditions would militate against their younger and lighter defenders. Their fears were well founded.

The game turned out to be a nightmare of the worst kind for Longford and the sight of their supporters streaming out of the ground with some twenty minutes still left to play underlined the one-sided nature of the exchanges. There was a huge gulf in class between the sides and only veteran Dessie Barry proved himself up to the task as Longford suffered a humiliating nineteen points trouncing.

The Midlanders desperately needed a forceful display from midfielders Enda Barden and Padraig Farrell to have any hope of causing a shock, but from very early on it became abundantly clear that the Offaly midfield pairing of Ciaran McManus and Ronan Mooney were in total control.

With the midfield battle won, Offaly forwards got plenty of possession and continually tormented the Longford backs who were unable to cope with their sheer power and pace.

Longford half-forward Trevor Smullen got the opening score of Championship '97 to put his side in front for the first and only time during the game. Although facing the breeze, Longford showed good promise in the opening ten minutes with some neat passing movements. But Offaly had moved into a 0-6 to 0-2 lead after 18 minutes and even at that early stage it looked a lost cause for Longford.

Colm Quinn struck for the first goal after 20 minutes and with all six forwards finding the target, Offaly had built up a commanding 1-11 to 0-4 lead approaching half-time. Longford were awarded a penalty some four minutes into injury-time after Niall Sheridan was fouled, but midfielder Enda Barden's low shot was scrambled out for a '45 by goalkeeper, Padraig Kelly. Any slim hope of a revival in Longford's fortunes was well and truly dashed.

A downpour at the start of the second-half hardly helped matters for Longford and once the impressive Roy Malone got Offaly's second goal five minutes after the re-start, only the final margin of victory remained to be resolved.

Further goals for Offaly from Anthony Kelly and Ciaran McManus, from a penalty, had the effect of sending disappointed Longford supporters scurrying towards the exits.

Vinny Claffey scored Offaly's fifth goal late in the game after a suicidal kick-out by Longford goalkeeper Gavin Tonra. Longford full-back Gary Brady appeared to slip and the unmarked Claffey could hardly believe his luck when the ball landed in his lap and he raced through to place it past the advancing Tonra to complete the rout.

Mighty Dessie Barry underlined his undoubted class with five points in the second half for Longford. Here is a man who has given his all for the county jersey with no tangible reward. Surely, a hero of renown. His immense contribution to Longford football since the early eighties should never be forgotten.

The players and officials in the Longford dressingroom were, naturally enough, very downhearted with the result. Manager Eamon Coleman was saying little although he did indicate to me that he 'was unlikely to stay on'. A few weeks later, the former Derry supremo decided to resign from his position to become the first management casualty of Championship '97.

Offaly manager Tommy Lyons made his way from the dressingroom across to the RTE commentary position and talked with me live on 'Sunday Sport' about the victory.

"We set out our stall very early on today and I thought we broke down Longford early in the game," Tommy said.

"We had a few goal chances in the first eight or ten minutes but we didn't take them and then Longford came into the game. Once we got to grips at midfield, we won the game comfortably. I thought the work-rate of our forwards was really the key to victory as they didn't allow the Longford backs out at all. That, in essence, was how we won the game today." When I asked him if we had just witnessed the 1997 Leinster Champions in action, he smiled and said, "We're the team to beat."

SCORERS - OFFALY: Anthony Kelly 1-3; Ciaran McManus 1-2; Roy Malone 1-2; Vinny Claffey 1-1; Colm Quinn 1-0; Peter Brady 0-3; Finbar Cullen 0-2; Ronan Mooney 0-1; Sean Grennan 0-1; James Grennan 0-1; Vincent Mooney 0-1
LONGFORD: Dessie Barry 0-6; Enda Barden 0-3; Eugene McCormack 0-3; Trevor Smullen 0-1

OFFALY

Padraig Kelly

Cathal Daly   Larry Carroll   James Brady
John Kenny   Finbar Cullen   Tom Coffey

Ciaran McManus   Ronan Mooney

Colm Quinn   Sean Grennan   Anthony Kelly
Peter Brady   Roy Malone   Vinny Claffey

SUBSTITUTES: James Grennan for Colm Quinn; David Foley for Cathal Daly; Vincent Mooney for Vinny Claffey;

LONGFORD

Gavin Tonra

Cathal Conefry   Gary Brady   Enda Ledwith
Colin Hannify   Ollie Reilly   Ciaran Keogh

Padraig Farrell   Enda Barden

Eugene McCormack   Trevor Smullen   Brendan Donoghue
Dessie Barry   Padraig Davis   Niall Sheridan

SUBSTITUTES: Frank McNamee for Ollie Reilly; John Hopkins for Ciaran Keogh; Ally McGahern for Padraig Farrell

OFFALY
BACK ROW L TO R: Larry Carroll, John Kenny, Seán Grennan, Ciaran McManus, Roy Malone, Vinny Claffey, Peter Brady, Cathal Daly;
FRONT ROW L TO R: Ronan Mooney, James Brady, Padraig Kelly, Finbar Cullen, Anthony Kelly, Tom Coffey, Colm Quinn.

LONGFORD
BACK ROW L TO R: Ciaran Keogh, Padraig Davis, Trevor Smullen, Niall Sheridan, Gavin Tonra, Gary Brady, Ollie Reilly, Enda Barden;
FRONT ROW L TO R: Padraig Farrell, Brendan Donohoe, Colin Hannify, Cathal Conefry, Enda Ledwith, Eugene McCormack.
(Dessie Barry missing from photograph)

SUNDAY, MAY 11, 1997

LEINSTER SENIOR FOOTBALL CHAMPIONSHIP PRELIMINARY ROUND

WEXFORD versus WESTMEATH

O'KENNEDY PARK, NEW ROSS

REFEREE: SEAMUS McCORMACK, MEATH

RESULT: WEXFORD 2-5 WESTMEATH 0-11 (A DRAW)

IMPRESSIVE wing-forward, Martin Flanagan, emerged as Westmeath's saviour when he scored an injury-time point from a high-pressure '45 to force a draw with Wexford in what was a free-ridden game at New Ross. Although their overall display was well below par, Westmeath showed great character to haul back a five points deficit in the last quarter to survive against the odds as Wexford failed to consolidate their strong position.

Referee Seamus McCormack booked no less than seven from each side in a tough and uncompromising game and also sent off Westmeath's Anthony Coyne and Wexford's Leigh O'Brien in separate incidents.

Coyne was first to receive his marching orders following an off-the-ball incident with Wexford's Richie Purcell after only eight minutes, while O'Brien was dismissed some thirteen minutes later for a foul on Paul Conway.

Wexford manager Cyril Hughes gave Championship debuts to defenders Darragh

Breen and Donal Redmond, midfielder Seamus Hughes and forward Garrett Dunne. The vastly experienced Scott Doran was unable to play because of injury and his place at right-corner-forward was taken by Jim Byrne.

Westmeath boss Barney Rock decided to include two of the 1995 All-Ireland-winning minor team, Kenny Mc Kinley and Thomas Cleary, while Kenny Lyons filled the vacant full-forward position.

Favourites Westmeath had a reasonably successful League campaign, finishing fourth in Division Three, while Wexford were relegated to Division Four. Indeed, so poor was Wexford's form, that the Slaneysiders emerged as the only team in all four divisions of the Church and General National Football League not to win a single game.

But League form usually counts for nothing in the cut and thrust of a championship game. And so it proved. Wexford, always hardy Championship campaigners, belied their lowly League position to turn in a gritty and determined performance that had Westmeath fighting for survival as the final whistle beckoned.

Leigh O'Brien got the scoring underway with two points for Wexford before Martin Flanagan opened Westmeath's account with a pointed free.

Wexford supporters were in full voice when Michael Mahon fired home the opening goal to move his side 1-2 to 0-1 ahead after fourteen minutes. Thomas Cleary responded with a point for Westmeath before O'Brien landed his third point for the home county. Soon afterwards, O'Brien was ordered-off and Westmeath took full advantage of his dismissal by finishing the half strongly with four unanswered points, including two from Kenny Lyons, to leave the sides level at the interval. One of Wexford's heroes in that opening half was goalkeeper John Cooper who denied Westmeath corner-forward Ger Heavin a certain goal with a point-blank save.

Wexford's decision to introduce substitute John O'Gorman at full-back paid dividends and the long-serving defender played a key role in tightening a less-than-assured defence. Midfielder John Harrington was outstanding all through for a Wexford side that certainly shook off the lethargy that enveloped them during the League.

The elusive Jason Lawlor evaded his marker to score Wexford's second goal which pushed the Slaneysiders five points clear, 2-5 to 0-6, after 52 minutes. But, inexplicably, Wexford failed to score again for the remainder of the game as the visitors found new life and vigour. Thomas Cleary landed two points from frees before a point each from Ger Heavin, Kenny Lyons and Martin Flanagan, from a '45 in injury-time, brought the game to a replay the following Saturday, May 17, in Mullingar.

Westmeath manager Barney Rock told me later that his team were fortunate to escape with a share of the spoils.

"We played very poorly, we know that. What spoiled it for us was the stop-start nature of the game. Wexford took their goal chances well and that kept them in the game. I was happy with the fact that we never gave up and Martin Flanagan did very well to score the equalising point. It certainly was a pressure kick and I was very relieved to see it go over the bar."

SCORERS - WEXFORD: Jason Lawlor 1-1; Leigh O'Brien 0-3; Michael Mahon 1-0; Barry Kirwan 0-1
WESTMEATH: Kenny Lyons 0-3; Martin Flanagan 0-3; Thomas Cleary 0-3; Ollie Keating 0-1;
Ger Heavin 0-1

WESTMEATH

Dermot Ryan

Dermot Brady | John O'Brien | Kenny McKinley

Ollie Keating | David Prendergast | John Cooney

Paul Conway | David Mitchell

Anthony Coyne | Thomas Cleary | Martin Flanagan

Christy McDonagh | Kenny Lyons | Ger Heavin

SUBSTITUTES: John Murray for Christy McDonagh;
Shane Colleary for David Mitchell; Mark Treanor for David Prendergast

WEXFORD

John Cooper

Donal Redmond | Paul Harrington | Darragh Breen

Willie Carley | Paddy Fitzhenry | Richie Purcell

John Harrington | Seamus Hughes

Leigh O'Brien | Barry Kirwan | Garrett Dunne

Jim Byrne | Michael Mahon | Jason Lawlor

SUBSTITUTES: John O'Gorman for Paul Harrington;
Rory Stafford for Mick Mahon; Des Stafford for Donal Redmond

WEXFORD
BACK ROW L TO R: Darragh Breen, Michael Mahon, John Harrington, Jim Byrne, Seamus Hughes, Donal Redmond, Garret Dunne, Paul Harrington;
FRONT ROW L TO R: Jason Lawlor, Paddy Fitzhenry, John Cooper, Barry Kirwan, Willie Carley, Richie Purcell, Leigh O'Brien.

WESTMEATH
BACK ROW L TO R: Ollie Keating, Thomas Cleary, Martin Flanagan, Kenny McKinley, Paul Conway, Anthony Coyne, John O'Brien, David Mitchell;
FRONT ROW L TO R: Ger Heavin, Christy McDonagh, Dermot Ryan, Dermot Brady, Kenny Lyons, David Prendergast, John Cooney.

SATURDAY, MAY 17, 1997

LEINSTER SENIOR FOOTBALL CHAMPIONSHIP PRELIMINARY ROUND (REPLAY)

WESTMEATH versus WEXFORD

CUSACK PARK, MULLINGAR

REFEREE: SEAMUS McCORMACK (MEATH)

RESULT: WESTMEATH 2-17 WEXFORD 1-15

WHAT A DIFFERENCE six days make!
The replay between football minnows Westmeath and Wexford turned out to be a hugely entertaining game devoid of the rancour that spoiled the drawn encounter. It was highly competitive and exciting with both sides displaying total commitment at all times on what was a perfect evening for football. It is always a pleasure to visit the newly refurbished Cusack Park in Mullingar which is a credit to everyone involved. The officials are extremely courteous and friendly and the commentary facilities for both national and regional radio networks are excellent. Westmeath were fortunate to earn a draw at New Ross six days earlier through an injury-time point from Martin Flanagan. The Tyrellspass player caused a mild scare in the dressingroom before the replay when he arrived with two left boots and had to borrow a pair from his half-forward colleague Shane Colleary.

Westmeath were forced to line-out without injured full-forward Kenny Lyons but Mark Staunton proved a very able replacement. Mullingar Shamrock's Tom Ormsby was also recalled in an effort to bolster the midfield sector. Captain Anthony Coyne was an absentee because of suspension. Manager Barney Rock was clearly unhappy with Westmeath's lethargic display in the drawn game, particularly the manner in which the Midlanders conceded two goals, and no doubt the genial 'Dub' made his displeasure known to his players.

Scott Doran returned to the Wexford line-up after missing the drawn encounter but free-taker Leigh O'Brien had to sit out the replay after his controversial dismissal the previous Sunday.

The game itself represented everything positive and enriching in gaelic football. Westmeath gave an assured and confident performance, but that was matched and at times surpassed by an equally impressive display by the visitors. Westmeath held the upperhand throughout and never once fell behind, but Cyril Hughes' team was always in contention and came within three points of the home side on no less than four occasions in the last quarter. Wexford simply refused to show the white flag and this contributed to a riveting encounter. High-fielding; some text book points; three goals and numerous flashes of brilliance, particularly from Westmeath's Ger Heavin, Ollie Keating and Mark Staunton, and Wexford's Scott Doran, Jim Byrne and Jason Lawlor, were just some of the ingredients that made this such a high quality game. Admittedly, there were times when players made elementary mistakes to remind us that, after all, we were watching two Division Three teams in action. But those occasions were rare!

Referee Seamus McCormack was authorative and decisive and deserves special mention for his confident handling of the game.

Ger Heavin scored the opening two points of the game for Westmeath and it was looking good for the Midlanders when midfielder Paul Conway got through for a well-taken goal after 11 minutes. Wexford drew level for the first and only time in the game when Scott Doran converted a penalty after 14 minutes' play.

Westmeath regained supremacy once more and outscored the Slaneysiders by 1-6 to 0-3 in the closing twenty-one minutes to lead at the interval by 2-8 to 1-5. Mark Staunton scored 1-1 during that purple patch, while Shane Collcary added two points, with Mark Treanor, John Murray and John Cooney adding a point each.

Westmeath had increased their lead to seven points by the 46th minute but again Wexford fought back courageously. Jim Byrne and Jason Lawlor were prominent in their revival and landed some superb points.

By the end of the third quarter, Wexford had reduced the deficit to three points and Westmeath appeared vulnerable. However, despite some gallant efforts, Wexford failed to score that all-important goal and Westmeath finished the stronger with late points from John Murray and Ger Heavin.

SCORERS - WESTMEATH: Mark Staunton 1-2; Thomas Cleary 0-4; Ger Heavin 0-3;
Paul Conway 1-0; Shane Collcary 0-2; Mark Treanor 0-2; John Murray 0-2;
Martin Flanagan 0-1; John Cooney 0-1;
WEXFORD: Jim Byrne 0-8; Jason Lawlor 0-4; Scott Doran 1-1; Niall Guinan 0-1; Garret Dunne 0-1

WESTMEATH

	Dermot Ryan	
Dermot Brady	John O'Brien	Kenny McKinley
Ollie Keating	John Murray	John Cooney
Tom Ormsby		Paul Conway
Thomas Cleary	Martin Flanagan	Shane Colleary
Ger Heavin	Mark Staunton	Mark Treanor

SUBSTITUTES: Kit Gillivan for Kenny McKinley;
David Mitchell for Dermot Brady; Damien Gavin for Shane Colleary;

WEXFORD

	Ollie Murphy	
Richie Purcell	John O'Gorman	Paddy Fitzhenry
Willie Carley	Barry Kirwan	Darragh Breen
John Harrington		Seamus Hughes
Jim Byrne	Niall Guinan	Garret Dunne
Scott Doran	John Roche	Jason Lawlor

SUBSTITUTES: Ronan Kinsella for Niall Guinan;
Michael Dunne for Barry Kirwan; Des Stafford for John O'Gorman

SUNDAY, MAY 25, 1997

LEINSTER SENIOR FOOTBALL CHAMPIONSHIP

OFFALY versus WESTMEATH

O'CONNOR PARK, TULLAMORE

REFEREE: PAT O'TOOLE, (LONGFORD)

RESULT: OFFALY 0-8 WESTMEATH 0-8 (A DRAW)

OVERWHELMING FAVOURITES Offaly came within seconds of being unceremoniously dumped out of the 1997 Championship by a Westmeath side that defied all the odds and were only denied victory by an injury-time point from Vinny Claffey. Westmeath had failed to beat Offaly in a senior Championship game since 1949, but surely there was never a time in those intervening years that the Midlanders had a better opportunity to put one over on their arch-rivals.

Westmeath had earned plaudits for the manner of their progress over the past twelve months and the two games against Wexford ensured the team was sharp, fit and focused. Manager Barney Rock expressed himself reasonably satisfied with his team's performance.

"I have always maintained that the longer a team remains in the Championship the better it becomes. Although we were missing some players through injury and suspension, we still had enough of the play to win the game."

Westmeath also had to make changes from their original selection when both Dermot Brady and Mark Treanor were declared unfit to play because of injury. David Mitchell replaced Brady at right-corner-back while Damien Gavin took over Treanor's place in the full-forward line.

Offaly, too, were forced to line-out without regular full-back Larry Carroll and he was replaced by Kevin Guing.

After an impressive victory over a weak Longford side in their previous round, nearly everyone expected high-flying Offaly to coast to victory against their near neighbours in the local derby.

Offaly manager Tommy Lyons felt his side showed commendable character to come back and force a replay.

"We missed an awful lot of chances and their goalkeeper, Dermot Ryan, brought off some outstanding saves. We did very well to come back and draw in the circumstances and we'll be going to Cusack Park in Mullingar determined to win the replay."

Westmeath never once trailed in a game where Offaly squandered numerous chances from eminently scorable positions. Midfielders Tom Ormsby and Paul Conway won an abundance of possession in the opening half and with Thomas Cleary finding the range from frees, Westmeath had built up a four points interval lead, 0-7 to 0-3. Six of those points came from placed kicks by Cleary while their only point from play in the entire game was scored by Jack Cooney midway through the opening half.

Although unlucky to hit the woodwork twice in the first half, Offaly rarely demonstrated the style and flair that were so evident in their clinical demolition of Longford in the previous round.

The 'Faithful County' supporters looked on in amazement as chance after chance was spurned after the interval. Westmeath goalkeeper Dermot Ryan was inspirational and he deprived Offaly of certain goals with two outstanding saves in the second half.

Vinny Claffey, Ronan Mooney and Ciaran McManus scored the opening three points of the second half to reduce the margin to a single point after 57 minutes. Westmeath's ace marksman, Cleary, landed his seventh pointed free to move his side two points clear with less than ten minutes remaining. Although it was Westmeath's only score of the second half, it proved a very valuable one. Claffey converted a free to leave the minimum between the sides and the Doon clubman landed the equaliser deep into injury-time to save Offaly's blushes.

Finbar Cullen was one of the all-too-few players on the Offaly team to enhance his reputation. Cullen was outstanding throughout and showed great leadership qualities at times of crisis.

Both sides displayed tremendous passion and commitment in pursuit of victory and the closeness of the exchanges ensured the drama continued right up until the final whistle.

Hard luck on Westmeath. A close call for Tommy Lyons' team. Next stop Cusack Park, Mullingar! One interesting feature of the game was the fact that only two players scored for Westmeath, the lowest number in the 1997 Football and Hurling Championships. Furthermore, no Westmeath forward scored from play and the Midlanders only scored once in the second half!

SCORERS - OFFALY: Vinny Claffey 0-4; Peter Brady 0-2; Ciaran McManus 0-1; Ronan Mooney 0-1
WESTMEATH: Thomas Cleary 0-7; John Cooney 0-1

OFFALY

Padraig Kelly

Cathal Daly	Kevin Guing	James Brady
John Kenny	Finbar Cullen	Tom Coffey
	Ciaran McManus / Ronan Mooney	
Colm Quinn	Sean Grennan	Anthony Kelly
Vinny Claffey	Roy Malone	Peter Brady

SUBSTITUTES: David Foley for Kevin Guing;
Vincent Mooney for Colm Quinn; James Grennan for Anthony Kelly

WESTMEATH

Dermot Ryan

David Mitchell	John O'Brien	Kenny McKinley
Ollie Keating	John Murray	John Cooney
	Tom Ormsby / Paul Conway	
Thomas Cleary	Martin Flanagan	Shane Colleary
Ger Heavin	Mark Staunton	Damien Gavin

SUBSTITUTES: Kit Gillivan for Damien Gavin; Christy McDonagh for Martin Flanagan

OFFALY
BACK ROW L TO R: James Brady, Peter Brady, Ronan Mooney, Ciaran McManus, Roy Malone, John Kenny, Seán Grennan, Kevin Guing;
FRONT ROW L TO R: Padraig Kelly, Vinny Claffey, Cathal Daly, Finbar Cullen, Anthony Kelly, Tom Coffey, Colm Quinn.

WESTMEATH
BACK ROW L TO R: John Murray, Ollie Keating, Mark Staunton, Shane Colleary, Martin Flanagan, Tom Ormsby, Paul Conway, John O'Brien, David Mitchell;
FRONT ROW L TO R: Ger Heavin, Thomas Cleary, Kenny McKinley, Damien Gavin, John Cooney, Dermot Ryan.

SUNDAY, JUNE 1, 1997

LEINSTER SENIOR FOOTBALL CHAMPIONSHIP QUARTER-FINAL

LOUTH versus CARLOW

ST. CONLETH'S PARK, NEWBRIDGE

REFEREE: JOHN BANNON, LONGFORD

RESULT: LOUTH 1-13 CARLOW 1-10

IT WAS AN UNUSUAL GAME! Carlow raced into an early four points lead but then could only muster a single point for the remainder of the first-half. Louth scored 1-6!

Same again, more or less, in the second-half. Carlow scored 1-1 in the opening four minutes and yet somehow could only manage a miserly one point in the course of the next half-hour. Louth helped themselves to seven points in the second-half but shot an unacceptable nine wides and almost paid the ultimate price for their wastefulness.

A courageous Carlow side, urged on by their astute manager, Bobby Millar, found new spirit in an extended injury-time period and scored three points without reply. Louth appeared vulnerable. Just a goal separated the sides. Carlow corner-forward Anthony 'Muckle' Keating had a great opportunity to level the game but his powerfully struck shot hit the side netting. A let-off for Louth. Not for the first time, goalkeeper Niall O'Donnell rescued the 'Wee County' with fine saves as Carlow frantically came in search of the equalising goal. O'Donnell's save from midfielder Seán Kavanagh was nail-biting stuff and Louth players and supporters alike were mightily relieved to hear the full-time whistle.

Favourites, Louth, physically stronger all round, had more than enough of the play to have won this game with something to spare and should not have had to rely on their brilliant keeper's sharp reflexes to save the day in those closing tension-filled minutes. The match lasted over 82 minutes. Longford referee John Bannon felt it necessary to allow a little over twelve minutes injury-time to take account of all the stoppages.

Louth manager, Paul Kenny, kindly made his way to the RTE Radio Commentary position in the Stand shortly after the game and talked with me live on Radio One. "I found it hard to understand why we missed so many good chances today," Paul said. "That's something we have to work on for the next game."

Ken Reilly and Seamus O'Hanlon gave Louth a distinct advantage at centre-field but their good work was too often negated by the poor scoring rate of their forwards.

Playing against the breeze, Carlow used the ball intelligently early on and scored four points without reply in the opening 11 minutes. Left-half-forward Pat Nolan accounted for two points in that period of dominance while Anthony Keating and Johnny Nevin scored a point each. Carlow could only manage one point for the rest of the first-half as Louth tightened their defence and O'Hanlon and Reilly began to exert their influence at midfield.

Carlow goalkeeper Pat Doran brought off a superb save from Brendan Kerin at the expense of a '45 which was converted by Colin Kelly after thirteen minutes to get Louth off the mark. Less than a minute later, full-forward Cathal O'Hanlon levelled matters with a well-taken goal. Alan Rooney, Aaron Hoey and corner-back Ray Rooney contributed a point each, while interprovincial star, Kelly, landed two further points from 45's to help Louth establish a four points lead, 1-6 to 0-5, at the interval.

Hoey stretched Louth's advantage almost immediately after the break with a pointed free before the impressive Willie Quinlan put Carlow right back in the hunt with a well-taken goal from a penalty after Anthony Keating was fouled. Soon afterwards, Keating himself landed a point from a free to bring Carlow within a single point of the favourites.

However, Carlow scored only one point over the next 32 minutes, during which time Louth added six points to build up what appeared an unassailable 1-13 to 1-7 lead with three minutes of normal time remaining. Louth won much more quality possession during that period but failed miserably to translate their territorial superiority to the scoreboard. Aaron Hoey was deprived a certain goal 17 minutes into the second-half after a magnificent save by Carlow substitute goalkeeper John Kearns, who had come on a little earlier in place of the injured Pat Doran.

Louth players appeared to be under the impression their work was done and were unable to cope with the unexpected onslaught from Carlow in the closing minutes. Substitute Hughie Brennan was a key figure in Carlow's revival. Keating scored two points and dual star Johnny Nevin added another to leave Carlow just two points adrift as the game moved into injury-time. Louth came close to paying a very heavy price for complacency in the latter stages and could well have had to face a replay but for the quick reflexes of their ever-reliable goalkeeper, Niall O'Donnell.

Carlow have now failed to beat Louth in their nine Championship meetings since 1950.

SCORERS - LOUTH: Colin Kelly 0-6; Cathal O'Hanlon 1-0; Alan Rooney 0-2; Aaron Hoey 0-2; Seamus O'Hanlon 0-1; Ray Rooney 0-1; Ollie McDonnell 0-1
CARLOW: Anthony Keating 0-5; Willie Quinlan 1-0; Johnny Nevin 0-2; Pat Nolan 0-2; Seán Kavanagh 0-1

LOUTH

Niall O'Donnell

Declan O'Sullivan | Gareth O'Neill | Ray Rooney
Gerry Curran | John Donaldson | Stephen Melia
Seamus O'Hanlon | Ken Reilly
Ollie McDonnell | Brendan Kerin | Alan Rooney
Aaron Hoey | Cathal O'Hanlon | Colin Kelly

SUBSTITUTE: David Reilly for Brendan Kerin

CARLOW

Pat Doran

Breffni Hannon | Andrew Corden | Shay Doorley
Joe Murphy | John Murphy | Brendan Hayden
Jody Morrissey | Seán Kavanagh
James O'Toole | Johnny Nevin | Pat Nolan
Willie Quinlan | Colm Hayden | Anthony Keating

SUBSTITUTES: Hughie Brennan for James O'Toole;
John Kearns for Pat Doran; Derek Treacy for John Murphy

LOUTH
BACK ROW L TO R: Brendan Kerin, Seamus O'Hanlon, Gareth O'Neill, Niall O'Donnell, John Donaldson, Stephen Melia, Gerry Curran, Ken Reilly;
FRONT ROW L TO R: Colin Kelly, Declan O'Sullivan, Aaron Hoey, Cathal O'Hanlon, Ray Rooney, Ollie McDonnell, Alan Rooney

CARLOW
BACK ROW L TO R: Colm Hayden, Breffni Hannon, Andrew Corden, Shay Doorley, Seán Kavanagh, Jody Morrissey, John Murphy, James O'Toole;
FRONT ROW L TO R: Joe Murphy, Brendan Hayden, Pat Doran, Willie Quinlan, Johnny Nevin, Anthony Keating, Pat Nolan.

SATURDAY, JUNE 7, 1997

LEINSTER SENIOR FOOTBALL CHAMPIONSHIP (REPLAY)

OFFALY versus WESTMEATH

CUSACK PARK, MULLINGAR

REFEREE: PAT O'TOOLE, LONGFORD

RESULT: OFFALY 1-14 WESTMEATH 0-7

Replays rarely follow the pattern of the drawn game and so it proved in this one-sided Championship tie as a completely transformed Offaly proved far too strong for a disappointing Westmeath team. Offaly were such impressive winners that it left one wondering how it could possibly be that practically the same team required an injury-time point to salvage a draw thirteen days earlier in Tullamore. Offaly certainly took advantage of their late reprieve and deservedly earned a Leinster quarter-final meeting with Wicklow in Croke Park.

Westmeath failed to reproduce their form of the drawn game as Offaly proceeded to dominate the game from early on and never once appeared in any danger of losing. Ciaran McManus and Ronan Mooney gave Offaly a distinct advantage at midfield while overall the team benefited immensely from Larry Carroll's return to the full-back line. Corner-back Cathal Daly, fast emerging as one of the finest defenders in the game, delivered another tour-de-force performance to shut out Westmeath's best efforts. The grit and determination so vital in tough Championship games was largely absent in an out-of-sorts Westmeath attack.

Conversely, the Offaly forward line, much maligned after the drawn game, had far too much power and mobility for an overstretched Westmeath defence. Vinny Claffey and Peter Brady were particularly prominent in the opening half and prospered from a consistent supply of good ball from midfield. David Reynolds punished any indescretions by the Westmeath defence with a splendid display of place kicking. The Clara marksman finished top scorer with six points. A valuable contribution.

Westmeath led briefly in the opening stages but once Offaly found their rhythm and Peter Brady found the net, only the margin of victory remained to be resolved. The goal stemmed from a superb pass by midfielder Ciaran McManus and the elusive Brady displayed his predatory instincts to put Offaly on the high road to victory.

Offaly held a six points advantage, 1-6 to 0-3, at the interval and Westmeath's misery continued immediately after the re-start when Jack Cooney's goal-bound shot was cleared off the line. Westmeath's challenge more or less petered out after that setback. Shortly afterwards, Westmeath goalkeeper Dermot Ryan brought off a magnificent save from Offaly full-forward Roy Malone.

Apart from Thomas Cleary, the Westmeath forwards had little success against a rock-solid Offaly defence and many of the Midlanders' best chances floundered in the Offaly half-back line.

Offaly had stretched their advantage to nine points, 1-9 to 0-3, within ten minutes of the re-start and thereafter the game deteriorated noticeably. Offaly were content to hold on to their lead while Westmeath, with a few exceptions, appeared to have little ambition to make their near neighbours work harder to earn their victory.

Offaly manager Tommy Lyons admitted afterwards that he had underestimated the intense rivalry that existed between the two counties in the drawn game. It was a valuable lesson and Offaly easily took the plaudits at the second attempt. It was a disappointing end to Westmeath's Championship campaign. Scoring forwards are essential if Westmeath footballers are to challenge for honours in the coming years!

SCORERS - OFFALY: David Reynolds 0-6; Peter Brady 1-2; Vinny Claffey 0-2; John Kenny 0-1; Ciaran McManus 0-1; Ronan Mooney 0-1; Mark Daly 0-1
WESTMEATH: Thomas Cleary 0-5; Paul Conway 0-1; Ger Heavin 0-1

OFFALY

	Padraig Kelly	
Cathal Daly	Larry Carroll	James Brady
John Kenny	Finbar Cullen	Tom Coffey
Ciaran McManus		Ronan Mooney
Colm Quinn	Sean Grennan	David Reynolds
Vinny Claffey	Roy Malone	Peter Brady

SUBSTITUTES: James Grennan for Seán Grennan; Mark Daly for Colm Quinn

WESTMEATH

Dermot Ryan

David Mitchell — John O'Brien — Dermot Brady

Ollie Keating — John Murray — John Cooney

Tom Ormsby — Paul Conway

Thomas Cleary — Martin Flanagan — Shane Colleary

Damien Gavin — Mark Staunton — Ger Heavin

SUBSTITUTES: Kenny McKinley for John Murray;
Mark Treanor for Mark Staunton; Kenny Lyons for Ger Heavin

OFFALY
BACK ROW L TO R: David Reynolds, Cathal Daly, Padraig Kelly, Seán Grennan, Larry Carroll, Roy Malone, Ciaran McManus, Ronan Mooney;
FRONT ROW L TO R: Peter Brady, James Brady, Vinny Claffey, John Kenny, Finbar Cullen, Tom Coffey, Colm Quinn.

WESTMEATH
BACK ROW L TO R: John Murray, Ollie Keating, Shane Colleary, Mark Staunton, Martin Flanagan, Tom Ormsby, John O'Brien, David Mitchell;
FRONT ROW L TO R: Ger Heavin, Thomas Cleary, Dermot Brady, Dermot Ryan, Damien Gavin, Paul Conway, John Cooney.

SUNDAY, JUNE 8, 1997

LEINSTER SENIOR FOOTBALL CHAMPIONSHIP QUARTER-FINAL

KILDARE versus LAOIS

CROKE PARK

REFEREE: PAT CASSERLY, WESTMEATH

RESULT: KILDARE 1-11 LAOIS 1-7

SALUTE THIRTEEN-MAN Kildare for the manner of their magnificent victory over League semi-finalists Laois against seemingly overwhelming odds. Mick O'Dwyer's Lilywhites, despite losing the services of two key forwards, Johnny McDonald and Martin Lynch, very early on, called on all their survival instincts to fashion a decisive victory that had their supporters dancing with delight at the final whistle.

Loyal Kildare football supporters have had precious little to get excited about in recent years, but all the pain of past defeats was washed away in a tide of euphoria as their courageous team overcame a surprisingly inept Laois side.

McDonald was sent-off following an off-the-ball foul on Laois corner-back Colm Burke after little more than nine minutes play, while Lynch was dismissed literally seconds later for his involvement in an incident with full-back Eamon Delaney. It was a first-ever sending-off for Lynch in his long career.

Following the two dismissals, shocked Kildare manager Mick O'Dwyer turned to his fellow selectors in despair and said: "We're going to get an almighty hammering here." Not a chance of it! Instead, thirteen brave Kildare players, inspired by their captain, Glen Ryan, chose to make a defiant statement that went a long way towards silencing some of their harshest critics. Mick O'Dwyer, the man who guided Kerry to eight All-Ireland titles from 1975 to 1986, patrolled the sideline non-stop issuing instructions to his players. He told me later that the victory compared favourably with any of his great achievements with his native Kerry, both as player and manager. Those sentiments summed up just how much O'Dwyer yearns to win major honours with Kildare.

Laois were unable to utilise their numerical advantage and super-fit Kildare thrived on a short-passing, running game that swept them to victory. The Laois management opted to keep their two extra players in defence, a ploy which backfired as Willie McCreery and Niall Buckley dominated midfield.

The sides were level at 0-1 apiece when McDonald and Lynch were ordered off, but Kildare made light of their obvious disadvantages and scored three points without reply. Laois corner-forward, Tom Bowe, levelled the match with a goal after 26 minutes but two points from accurate free-taker Padraig Graven, in reply to a point from play by David Sweeney, left Kildare 0-6 to 1-2 ahead at the interval.

Glen Ryan was outstanding at centre-half-back for Kildare and it was only fitting that he converted a vital penalty six minutes into the second-half. With regular penalty taker Martin Lynch out-of-bounds, the Kildare captain confidently struck the ball past Laois goalkeeper, Fergal Byron, to stretch the 'Lilywhites' lead to five points. Ian Fitzgerald converted two frees to reduce the margin as Laois tried desperately to retrieve the game. However, Kildare always held the upperhand and Laois never closed the gap to less than three points in the remaining free-ridden twenty-one minutes. Kildare goalkeeper Christy Byrne brought off a superb save from Denis Lalor in the closing minutes to deprive Laois a badly-needed goal. Byrne had an outstanding game and must surely rate as one of the finest goalkeepers in the game.

Every Kildare player was a hero, although none more so than Eddie McCormack, who tormented the Laois defence throughout; Championship debutant, Padraig Graven, converted eight points from frees while towering captain, Glen Ryan, once again displayed his undoubted leadership qualities with a 'Man-Of-The-Match' performance. Round Towers player, Ryan, scored 1-2 and was particularly impressive.

Laois conceded close to fifty frees in the course of the game and that statistic alone underlined the panicky nature of their play. This is a game Laois will want to forget as far too many of their players failed to perform when it mattered most. To compound their misfortune, David Sweeney, one of their better players on the day, was ordered off late in the game.

SCORERS - KILDARE: Padraig Graven 0-8; Glen Ryan 1-2; Niall Buckley 0-1
LAOIS: Tom Bowe 1-1; Ian Fitzgerald 0-3; David Sweeney 0-2; Leo Turley 0-1

KILDARE

Christy Byrne

Davy Dalton — Ronan Quinn — Sos Dowling

Anthony Rainbow — Glen Ryan — Ken Doyle

Niall Buckley — Willie McCreery

Eddie McCormack — Declan Kerrigan — Tom Harris

Padraig Graven — Martin Lynch — Johnny McDonald

SUBSTITUTES: Martin Ryan for Tom Harris

LAOIS

Fergal Byron

Colm Burke — Eamonn Delaney — Adrian Phelan

Denis Lalor — Derek Conroy — Martin Delaney

Tony Maher — David Sweeney

Ian Fitzgerald — P. J. Dempsey — Michael Lawlor

Tom Bowe — Hughie Emerson — Leo Turley

SUBSTITUTES: Damien Ryan for Colm Burke; Kevin Fitzpatrick for Michael Lawlor

KILDARE
BACK ROW L TO R: Willie McCreery, Niall Buckley, Martin Lynch, Christy Byrne, Davy Dalton, Anthony Rainbow, Padraig Graven, Ronan Quinn;
FRONT ROW L TO R: Ken Doyle, Declan Kerrigan, Glen Ryan, Sos Dowling, Eddie McCormack, Tom Harris, Johnny McDonald.

LAOIS
BACK ROW L TO R: Leo Turley, David Sweeney, Colm Burke, Fergal Byron, Derek Conroy, Denis Lalor, Eamonn Delaney, Tony Maher;
FRONT ROW L TO R: Adrian Phelan, Michael Lawlor, Hughie Emerson, P.J. Dempsey, Tom Bowe, Ian Fitzgerald, Martin Delaney.

SUNDAY, JUNE 15, 1997

LEINSTER SENIOR FOOTBALL CHAMPIONSHIP QUARTER-FINAL

OFFALY versus WICKLOW

CROKE PARK

REFEREE: PAUL MCGANN (WESTMEATH)

RESULT: OFFALY 1-17 WICKLOW 1-8

EACH NEW GAME BRINGS new challenges and each new day Offaly footballers pass yet another test with commendable style and flair on their way back to the lofty heights of the early Eighties.

Inspirational manager Tommy Lyons deserves every credit for assembling a team with the potential to make a major breakthrough in the very near future.

The game against Wicklow underlined just how much Offaly have improved since last years's first-round Championship exit against Louth, and also provided a fairly accurate barometer of what is now required to make further headway in Championship '97.

Offaly benefitted enormously from their three games in the Championship and were always in control against an inept Wicklow side that struggled in far too many areas. The Offaly forward-line was impressive throughout and from the time Peter Brady scored his first point, it became clear the Wicklow defence would need to sharpen up if the Division Four champions were to be held at bay. The signs were ominous for Wicklow by the manner in which Offaly, favoured by the breeze, powered their way into a commanding 0-5 to 0-1 lead after just 12 minutes. Earlier, Wicklow goalkeeper, Liam Cullen, saved brilliantly from Roy Malone.

Ciaran McManus and Seán Grennan each scored a splendid point from play in that early period of Offaly dominance which was no more than their strong and forceful play deserved.

But, not for the first time, full-forward Kevin O'Brien hauled Wicklow right back into the game with a goal of the highest quality. The former All-Star gathered the ball inside the Offaly 45 metre line and left Larry Carroll trailing as he set off on a solo run before despatching the ball to the net past goalkeeper Padraig Kelly. Conan Daye equalised soon after before Seán Grennan and Damien McMahon exchanged points to level the game for the third time, 0-6 to 1-3, after eighteen minutes.

O'Brien's goal, Cullen's save and Fergus Daly's high-fielding failed to lift Wicklow and a Peter Brady goal helped Offaly establish a comfortable 1-10 to 1-3 half-time lead.

Wicklow lost their only real chance to keep the game alive 13 minutes after the restart when right-half-forward, Keith Byrne, shot wide from a penalty after goalkeeper, Padraig Kelly, had fouled the ever threatening Kevin O'Brien.

That penalty miss totally deflated Wicklow and resurgent Offaly took control and scored six points without reply to surge twelve points clear. Offaly appeared to sit back and admire a job well done in the closing stages and Wicklow took advantage of the slight reprieve and scored three late points.

SCORERS - OFFALY: David Reynolds 0-7; Peter Brady 1-3; Seán Grennan 0-3; Vinny Claffey 0-2; Ciaran McManus 0-1; Mark Daly 0-1

WICKLOW: Conan Daye 0-3; Kevin O'Brien 1-0; Damien McMahon 0-2; Jonathan Behan 0-1; Seamus Miley 0-1; Shane O'Neill 0-1

OFFALY

Padraig Kelly

Cathal Daly — Larry Carroll — James Brady

John Kenny — Finbar Cullen — Tom Coffey

Ciaran McManus — Ronan Mooney

Colm Quinn — Sean Grennan — David Reynolds

Peter Brady — Roy Malone — Vinny Claffey

SUBSTITUTES: Mark Daly for Colm Quinn; Vincent Mooney for Peter Brady; David Foley for James Brady

WICKLOW

Liam Cullen

Barry O'Donovan — Hugh Kenny — Brendán Ó hAnnaidh

Seamus Miley — Philip McGillycuddy — Brian Whelan

Fergus Daly — Raymond Danne

Keith Byrne — Stephen Byrne — Jonathan Behan

Damien McMahon — Kevin O'Brien — Conan Daye

SUBSTITUTES: Mick Murtagh for Philip McGillycuddy; Shane O'Neill for Stephen Byrne; Seamus Nolan for Jonathan Behan

OFFALY

BACK ROW L TO R: Colm Quinn, Ronan Mooney, David Reynolds, John Kenny, Seán Grennan, Roy Malone, Larry Carroll, Ciaran McManus;

FRONT ROW L TO R: James Brady, Cathal Daly, Peter Brady, Finbar Cullen, Padraig Kelly, Vinny Claffey, Tom Coffey.

WICKLOW
BACK ROW L TO R: Hugh Kenny, Seamus Miley, Brendan Ó hAnnaidh, Raymond Danne, Stephen Byrne, Fergus Daly, Philip McGillycuddy;
FRONT ROW L TO R: Conan Daye, Barry O'Donovan, Jonathan Behan, Keith Byrne, Liam Cullen, Brian Whelan, Damien McMahon, Kevin O'Brien.

SUNDAY, JUNE 15, 1997

LEINSTER SENIOR FOOTBALL CHAMPIONSHIP QUARTER-FINAL

MEATH versus DUBLIN

CROKE PARK

REFEREE: BRIAN WHITE (WEXFORD)

RESULT: MEATH 1-13 DUBLIN 1-10

THIS WAS THE GAME that set the Football Championship alight - an enthralling game that was as full of passion, commitment and raw courage as any of the encounters in that epic four-match series of 1991. It was a typical Dublin - Meath clash!

There was nothing spared in endeavour and the tension was almost unbearable as first Meath took control and then Dublin rallied with telling effect. And then it all came down to the last kick of the game! With the stop-watch ticking into injury-time, Meath full-back, Darren Fay, was penalised for a foot block as Mick Galvin shot for goal and Wexford referee Brian White had no hesitation in awarding a penalty.

But much to the dismay of Dublin players and supporters alike, Paul Bealin's powerfully struck shot cannoned off the underside of the crossbar and Dublin were out of Championship '97 in the cruellest way possible. How often in the past have meetings between the two kingpins of Leinster turned out to be thrillers of Hitchcockian proportions? This was no exception!

Meath won this game simply because their players were better equipped to take scores. Of the six Dublin forwards that started the game, only right-half-forward Jim

Gavin scored from play. In stark contrast, all Meath's six forwards, along with midfielders, John McDermott and Jimmy McGuinness, found the target from play in a potent twenty-five minute spell in the first-half.

Dublin raced into a 0-3 to 0-1 lead after ten minutes with two points from Charlie Redmond and one from midfielder Brian Stynes, but soon lost the momentum as Meath got on about their business with the style of champions. That early phase proved very productive for Dublin. Paul Bealin and Stynes were performing exceptionally well at midfield while Dessie Farrell and Jason Sherlock were both very prominent in the forward line.

But then came a quite astonishing turnaround. Meath outscored the Dubs by 1-9 to 0-1 over the next 24 minutes in an awesome display of point scoring. John McDermott and Jimmy McGuinness reversed the trend at midfield and scored a point each to kick-start Meath's challenge. Further 'top of the range' points from Brendan Reilly, Evan Kelly, Trevor Giles, Graham Geraghty and Ollie Murphy pushed the All-Ireland champions 0-8 to 0-3 ahead after 26 minutes. Another point from the impressive Giles put Meath further ahead before Jim Gavin landed a point for Dublin - their first score for over eighteen minutes.

There was further misery for the beleaguered Dubs defence when Ollie Murphy palmed the ball to the net past John O'Leary. It was a scenario of nightmare porportions for Dublin and there appeared no possible avenue whatsoever in which to escape. Meath were rampant and the Dubs were on the ropes! But before the All-Ireland champions could deliver the knock-out blow, shell-shocked Dublin hit back with a vengeance.

Manager Mickey Whelan sent on the adventurous Mick Deegan to try and rescue a sinking ship. The Erin's Isle 'pocket rocket' made an instant impact and Dublin's revival coincided with his introduction. Eamonn Heery, Keith Barr and Paul Curran took matters into their own hands and surged forward at every opportunity. Dublin threw caution to the wind and it paid off handsomely. Keith Barr finished a sweeping movement involving Deegan, Curran and Farrell by crashing the ball past Conor Martin for a wonder Dublin goal. Stynes and Bealin were back on top again at midfield and Meath backs were finding it difficult to stop the flow. Heery and Stynes landed a point apiece before half-time to reduce the margin to just four points.

It was an equally amazing second-half but Dublin's inability to convert their chances proved extremely costly. Stynes was superb at midfield and the Dublin forwards got much more supply but were unable to make much headway against a strong and resolute Meath defence in which Darren Fay and Mark O'Reilly were outstanding. Nigel Nestor, Enda McManus and Donal Curtis all performed heroically in the face of adversity.

Dublin twice came within one point of Meath in an absorbing second-half that saw the All-Ireland champions tested to the limit. Trevor Giles shot wide from a penalty after 48 minutes as Meath struggled to regain the initiative. When Brendan Reilly landed a second-half point after 63 minutes, it was Meath's first score for nearly half an hour. Dublin failed to capitalise on a vast amount of possession and shot nine wides in the second-half. As the tide began to turn, John McDermott scored a fine point and another from Tommy Dowd stretched Meath's advantage to three points. Although Dowd's point was to be the final score of the game, it was a missed penalty that determined which of the 'Big Two' advanced to meet Kildare in the semi-final. Meath prevailed in a very sporting game but only by the width of a crossbar!

SCORERS - MEATH: Ollie Murphy 1-1; Trevor Giles 0-3; John McDermott 0-2; Tommy Dowd 0-2; Brendan Reilly 0-2; Evan Kelly 0-1; Jimmy McGuinness 0-1; Graham Geraghty 0-1
DUBLIN: Charlie Redmond 0-4; Keith Barr 1-0; Brian Stynes 0-2; Jim Gavin 0-1; Paul Curran 0-1; Eamonn Heery 0-1; Peter Ward 0-1

MEATH

Conor Martin

Mark O'Reilly — Darren Fay — Colm Coyle

Nigel Nestor — Enda McManus — Donal Curtis

Jimmy McGuinness — John McDermott

Evan Kelly — Trevor Giles — Graham Geraghty

Tommy Dowd — Brendan Reilly — Ollie Murphy

SUBSTITUTES: Jody Devine for Evan Kelly

DUBLIN

John O'Leary

Paddy Christie — Ian Robertson — Ciaran Walsh

Paul Curran — Keith Barr — Eamonn Heery

Brian Stynes — Paul Bealin

Jim Gavin — Dessie Farrell — Paul Clarke

Jason Sherlock — Mick Galvin — Charlie Redmond

SUBSTITUTES: Mick Deegan for Paul Clarke;
Peter Ward for Jim Gavin; Paddy Moran for Ciaran Walsh

MEATH
BACK ROW L TO R: Trevor Giles, Graham Geraghty, John McDermott, Jimmy McGuinness, Tommy Dowd, Brendan Reilly, Nigel Nestor;
FRONT ROW L TO R: Donal Curtis, Mark O'Reilly, Ollie Murphy, Colm Coyle, Evan Kelly, Conor Martin, Darren Fay, Enda McManus.

DUBLIN
BACK ROW L TO R: Charlie Redmond; Mick Galvin, Ian Robertson, Paddy Christie, Paul Bealin, Brian Stynes, Ciaran Walsh, Keith Barr;
FRONT ROW L TO R: Paul Clarke, Jason Sherlock, Jim Gavin, Dessie Farrell, Paul Curran, John O'Leary, Eamonn Heery.

SUNDAY, JUNE 29, 1997

LEINSTER SENIOR FOOTBALL CHAMPIONSHIP SEMI-FINAL

OFFALY versus LOUTH

PAIRC TAILTEANN, NAVAN

REFEREE: JOHN BANNON (LONGFORD)

RESULT: OFFALY 1-10 LOUTH 0-11

THE FOURTEEN-YEAR WAIT is over! Offaly supporters celebrated as their county footballers advanced to a first provincial decider since their shock defeat by eventual All-Ireland Champions Dublin back in 1983.

It was a largely uninspiring game at Páirc Tailteann and fell someway short of matching the drama of the game between Meath and Dublin two weeks previously.

Make no mistake, this was a wonderful victory for Offaly and great credit is due to their manager Tommy Lyons for the manner in which he masterminded their march to the Leinster Final.

Louth were bitterly disappointed to lose after such high expectations of reaching a long overdue first Leinster Final since 1960, but their late rally which yielded four unanswered points was not sufficient to deny Offaly a deserved victory.

Louth were dealt a cruel blow just before the start when their star midfielder and captain, Seamus O'Hanlon, aggravated an achilles tendon shortly before the game and was unable to line out. O'Hanlon's absence upset the balance of the whole team. Offaly started sluggishly and had just two points on the board after 30 minutes play but a goal from Seán Grennan followed by a point each from David Reynolds and Vinny Claffey in the closing stages of the first-half helped the Midlanders establish a 1-4 to 0-4 interval advantage. Although their forwards got much less possession in the first-half than their Louth counterparts, Offaly availed of the limited opportunities that came their way while Louth proceeded to fritter away far too many gilt-edged chances. Offaly's game plan to curb the threat of O'Hanlon was thrown into disarray when the Clan na Gael club man failed to take his place in the starting line-up. Offaly midfielders struggled for long periods of the first-half but there was a marked improvement in that sector after the break.

Cathal O'Hanlon and Ollie McDonnell landed a point each for Louth early in the second-half, but it soon emerged that Offaly's forwards had the measure of a less than confident Louth defence. Impressive free-taker, David Reynolds, scored four points from frees while the supremely confident Roy Malone tacked on two further points from play in a twelve-minute purple-patch. Louth staged a late comeback in a desperate attempt to salvage the game. Half-back Stephen Melia surged forward to score a point, while substitute Stefan White fired over two excellent points from play as Louth narrowed the gap in the closing, tension-filled minutes. Louth half-forward Ollie McDonnell scored the final point of the game, but by then Offaly had their work complete and were back in a provincial football final for the first time in fourteen years.

SCORERS - OFFALY: David Reynolds 0-7; Seán Grennan 1-0; Roy Malone 0-2; Vinny Claffey 0-1
LOUTH: Cathal O'Hanlon 0-3; Ollie McDonnell 0-2; Stefan White 0-2; Colin Kelly 0-2; Brendan Kerin 0-1; Stephen Melia 0-1

OFFALY

Padraig Kelly

Barry Malone — Larry Carroll — Cathal Daly

John Kenny — Finbar Cullen — Tom Coffey

Ciaran McManus — Ronan Mooney

Mark Daly — Sean Grennan — David Reynolds

Vinny Claffey — Roy Malone — Peter Brady

SUBSTITUTES: Colm Quinn for Mark Daly

LOUTH

Niall O'Donnell

Declan O'Sullivan — Gareth O'Neill — Ray Rooney

Gerry Curran — John Donaldson — Stephen Melia

Brendan Kerin — Ken Reilly

Ollie McDonnell — David Reilly — Alan Rooney

Colin Kelly — Cathal O'Hanlon — Pat Butterly

SUBSTITUTES: Stefan White for Pat Butterly; Nicky Malone for Brendan Kerin; Martin Farrelly for Colin Kelly

OFFALY

BACK ROW L TO R: Larry Carroll, Cathal Daly, Seán Grennan, Ciaran McManus, Ronan Mooney, Roy Malone, John Kenny, David Reynolds;

FRONT ROW L TO R: Peter Brady, Tom Coffey, Mark Daly, Barry Malone, Finbar Cullen, Padraig Kelly, Vinny Claffey.

LOUTH

BACK ROW L TO R: Declan O'Sullivan, John Donaldson, Stephen Melia, Gerry Curran, Niall O'Donnell, Gareth O'Neill, Seamus O'Hanlon, Ken Reilly;

FRONT ROW L TO R: Ray Rooney, Pat Butterly, Cathal O'Hanlon, Ollie McDonnell, David Reilly, Alan Rooney, Colin Kelly.

SUNDAY, JULY 6, 1997

LEINSTER SENIOR FOOTBALL CHAMPIONSHIP SEMI-FINAL

MEATH versus KILDARE

CROKE PARK

REFEREE: PAT O'TOOLE (LONGFORD)

RESULT: MEATH 0-12 KILDARE 1-9 (A DRAW)

ALL-IRELAND CHAMPIONS Meath survived to fight another day in a highly-competitive game that had both sets of supporters on tenterhooks right up until the final whistle. Kildare travelled to Croke Park absolutely intent on winning this semi-final clash, and Mick O'Dwyer's brave warriors were somewhat unlucky not to accomplish their mission. Niall Buckley had a glorious chance to clinch victory for the Lilywhites near the very end, but his '45 metre free dropped short and was gathered by towering midfielder, John McDermott.

Meath are becoming masters at living dangerously and then against the odds somehow snatching late draws or narrow wins. Consider this! Meath drew with Mayo courtesy of a last minute point from Colm Coyle in last year's All-Ireland final while Brendan Reilly kicked the winning point in the replay.

Meath survived against Dublin in the first round this year when Paul Bealin's penalty kick crashed off the crossbar. It was the last kick of the game and Meath marched on! Just when it appeared the champions had run out of luck against Kildare, Trevor Giles came to their rescue with a magnificent equalising point in the closing minutes. Talk about living on the edge!

Meath were never ahead in a game in which Kildare had more than sufficient chances to take the spoils. But their short passing game let them down on occasions when a quick and well directed ball into the full-forward line might have reaped better rewards.

Graham Geraghty, Tommy Dowd and Trevor Giles were the pick of the Meath forwards and scored valuable points at crucial stages of the game. Dowd kicked over Meath's opening point; Geraghty added two points early in the second-half, while Giles delivered the equalising score under pressure. The trio accounted for eight points of Meath's total.

Kildare matched the All-Ireland champions in all facets of play and afterwards manager Mick O'Dwyer expressed himself satisfied with the manner in which his players acquitted themselves in what was an unremitting encounter. Meath, too, performed heroics to stave off defeat on a day when a good many of their team surprisingly played below par. Expect Meath to be much sharper in the replay!

Kildare got off to a lightning start with a goal from full-forward Martin Lynch after less than one minute of action. Kildare held that goal advantage at half-time but two excellent points from an in-form Geraghty and another magnificent point from Jimmy McGuinness shortly after the re-start brought the sides level for the first time.

It was a real test for Kildare and Padraig Graven answered the call with two pointed frees before Geraghty and Declan Kerrigan exchanged points.

Meath battled tenaciously to draw level for the second time in the game with a point each from Ollie Murphy and Giles. The game was now on a knife-edge! On another day, Kildare might have capitulated under the intense pressure. Not so this time! Instead Declan Kerrigan edged the Lilywhites ahead with a splendid point seven minutes from time. Typically, Meath continued to dig deep to salvage the game and their relief was palpable when Giles kicked over the levelling point.

SCORERS - MEATH: Trevor Giles 0-4; Graham Geraghty 0-3; Jimmy McGuinness 0-2; Tommy Dowd 0-1; Brendan Reilly 0-1; Ollie Murphy 0-1
KILDARE: Padraig Graven 0-3; Martin Lynch 1-0; Declan Kerrigan 0-2; Niall Buckley 0-1; Anthony Rainbow 0-1; Willie McCreery 0-1; Eddie McCormack 0-1

MEATH

Conor Martin

Mark O'Reilly — Darren Fay — Donal Curtis

Colm Coyle — Enda McManus — Nigel Nestor

Jimmy McGuinness — John McDermott

Trevor Giles — Tommy Dowd — Graham Geraghty

Evan Kelly — Brendan Reilly — Ollie Murphy

SUBSTITUTES: Paddy Reynolds for Nigel Nestor; P.J. Gillic for Evan Kelly

KILDARE

Christy Byrne

Davy Dalton — Ronan Quinn — Sos Dowling

Anthony Rainbow — Glen Ryan — Ken Doyle

Niall Buckley — Willie McCreery

Eddie McCormack — Declan Kerrigan — Tom Harris

Padraig Graven — Martin Lynch — Johnny McDonald

SUBSTITUTES: Martin Ryan for Ronan Quinn; Dermot Earley for Johnny McDonald

MEATH
BACK ROW L TO R: Trevor Giles, Graham Geraghty, John McDermott, Jimmy McGuinness, Brendan Reilly, Tommy Dowd, Nigel Nestor;
FRONT ROW L TO R: Colm Coyle, Donal Curtis, Mark O'Reilly, Ollie Murphy, Conor Martin, Evan Kelly, Darren Fay, Enda McManus.

KILDARE
BACK ROW L TO R: Martin Lynch, Willie McCreery, Niall Buckley, Christy Byrne, Davy Dalton, Anthony Rainbow, Padraig Graven, Ronan Quinn;
FRONT ROW L TO R: Johnny McDonald, Ken Doyle, Glen Ryan, Eddie McCormack, Sos Dowling, Tom Harris, Declan Kerrigan.

SUNDAY, JULY 20, 1997

LEINSTER SENIOR FOOTBALL CHAMPIONSHIP SEMI-FINAL (REPLAY)

MEATH versus KILDARE

CROKE PARK

REFEREE: PAT O'TOOLE (LONGFORD)

RESULT: MEATH 2-20 KILDARE 3-17 (AFTER EXTRA-TIME)

ALL-IRELAND CHAMPIONS Meath several times stared defeat in the face, but once again, in Houdini-like fashion, Seán Boylan's young cavaliers somehow survived against what appeared to be insurmountable odds. 1996 Footballer Of The Year Trevor Giles scored the equalising point in the first game, and the same player produced a match-saving goal to send this replay into extra-time. But Kildare appeared to have guaranteed themselves victory when they led by six points at the end of the first period of extra-time.

What followed almost defied belief. Rejuvenated Meath, calling on all their survival instincts, staged an astonishing comeback which yielded no fewer than seven points without reply. Super sub Jody Devine scored four spectacular points from play to turn the tide decisively in favour of the champions. Then, somehow, Kildare rallied and substitute Paul McCormack fisted over the levelling point in an extended period of injury-time.

It was the day two substitutes, unsung heroes Devine and McCormack, made their marks; it was the day of five goals; forty-two scores; the day Trevor Giles scored a penalty, missed another, and still finished with an incredible tally of 2-8; it was the day of

Graham Geraghty's sending off and the retirement of match referee Pat O'Toole because of cramp. Fellow Longford referee John Bannon deputised. Truly an epic that evoked memories of the Meath/Dublin four-game saga of 1991. Football was the clear and unequivocal winner. The one absolute certainty about the second replay is that superglue will be the only effective way to keep the sell-out crowd on their seats.

Kildare had sufficient chances to win on both occasions, but guess what, Meath are still there. And fighting fit!

Kildare manager Mick O'Dwyer felt it was one of the best games ever for the sheer commitment and dedication of both teams. "We were probably slightly the better team the first day, but a team of the calibre of Meath are very difficult to beat. I can't ever remember seeing anything like this replay. The speed of the game was unreal. I heard people saying that mistakes were made, but of course mistakes will be made when you play the game at that speed. The players are gambling all the time and throwing caution to the wind."

Meath are renowned for their never-say-die attitude and that trait was never more in evidence than in this game. The All-Ireland Champions looked in deep trouble when they trailed by five points early in the second-half and then by no less than six at the end of the first period of extra-time.

Both sets of players were emotionally and physically drained at the finish of what was a pulsating encounter. Star Kildare midfielder Niall Buckley got into his stride from early on and picked off the first point. From there to the final whistle, the Lilywhites fought the good fight against the might of the All-Ireland Champions. Left-half-forward Tom Harris got the vital touch to score the opening goal of the game after 21 minutes to push Kildare 1-3 to 0-4 ahead. Two points from Padraig Graven and a point from Martin Lynch extended that lead further. Meath replied with a point from Brendan Reilly and two from Trevor Giles before Eddie McCormack, outstanding all through, got his name on the scoresheet with a fine point to leave Kildare ahead 1-7 to 0-7 at half-time.

Buckley stretched Kildare's lead with a point early in the second-half but yet again the game took another twist. Tommy Dowd, Brendan Reilly and Giles all found the target and now the All-Ireland Champions were just one point adrift.

It was a thrill a minute from there to the finish: Brian Murphy scored a superb goal for Kildare; Eddie McCormack landed a point; Giles converted a penalty and Graham Geraghty was sent off for a foul on Glen Ryan. Kildare were leading by three points entering the final minutes when Dowd won a penalty but Giles's effort was saved by Christy Byrne. And then another twist! Ollie Murphy's sideline ball was palmed to the net by the brilliant Giles. An exceptional player!

The extra-time that followed matched anything ever before witnessed at a major Championship game in Croke Park.

Kildare scored 1-3 without reply in the first-half of extra-time at the end of which the All-Ireland Champions looked a spent force. But write-off Meath at your peril. One day Tommy Dowd will do the damage and defy logic; another day Trevor Giles will turn the game around; John McDermott is also well capable of taking up the mantle and some other time Brendan Reilly will play the starring role. And so on and on! Meath are never short of finding heroes when the need is greatest. And they found one again in the second period of extra-time. Faithful son of Meath, Jody Devine, took the game by the scruff of the neck and scored four spectacular points from play as Meath came storming back like men possessed. Seven unanswered points and incredibly the All-Ireland Champions were back in front for the first time since midway through the first-half of normal time. Now it was Kildare's turn to feel the cold shiver of defeat. But not for long. Substitute Paul McCormack saved the day with a fisted point. Drama to the very end.

SCORERS - MEATH: Trevor Giles 2-8; Jody Devine 0-4; Brendan Reilly 0-3; Ollie Murphy 0-2; Tommy Dowd 0-2; Graham Geraghty 0-1
KILDARE: Padraig Graven 0-6; Eddie McCormack 0-4; Niall Buckley 0-4; Brian Murphy 1-0; Tom Harris 1-0; Willie McCreery 1-0: Martin Lynch 0-1; Dermot Earley 0-1; Paul McCormack 0-1

MEATH

Conor Martin

Mark O'Reilly | Darren Fay | Donal Curtis

Paddy Reynolds | Enda McManus | Colm Coyle

Jimmy McGuinness | John McDermott

Trevor Giles | Tommy Dowd | Graham Geraghty

P.J. Gillic | Brendan Reilly | Ollie Murphy

SUBSTITUTES: Martin O'Connell for Enda McManus;
Nigel Nestor for Jimmy McGuinness; Jody Devine for P.J. Gillic;
EXTRA-TIME: Evan Kelly for Graham Geraghty (sent-off in normal time)
Jimmy McGuinness for Colm Coyle; Enda McManus for Mark O'Reilly;
Kevin Cahill for Jimmy McGuinness

KILDARE

Christy Byrne

Martin Ryan | Davy Dalton | Sos Dowling

Anthony Rainbow | Glen Ryan | Ken Doyle

Niall Buckley | Willie McCreery

Eddie McCormack | Declan Kerrigan | Tom Harris

Padraig Graven | Martin Lynch | Brian Murphy

SUBSTITUTES: Dermot Earley for Willie McCreery;
Brian Fahy for Tom Harris; Paul McCormack for Ken Doyle

MEATH

BACK ROW L TO R: Trevor Giles, Graham Geraghty, John McDermott, Tommy Dowd, P.J. Gillic, Brendan Reilly, Jimmy McGuinness; FRONT ROW L TO R: Colm Coyle, Donal Curtis, Mark O'Reilly, Ollie Murphy, Conor Martin, Darren Fay, Paddy Reynolds, Enda McManus.

KILDARE

BACK ROW L TO R: Brian Murphy, Martin Lynch, Niall Buckley, Willie McCreery, Davy Dalton, Anthony Rainbow, Martin Ryan, Padraig Graven;
FRONT ROW L TO R: Ken Doyle, Eddie McCormack, Glen Ryan, Christy Byrne, Sos Dowling, Tom Harris, Declan Kerrigan.

SUNDAY, AUGUST 3, 1997

LEINSTER SENIOR FOOTBALL CHAMPIONSHIP SEMI-FINAL
(SECOND REPLAY)

MEATH versus KILDARE

CROKE PARK

REFEREE: PAT O'TOOLE (LONGFORD)

RESULT: MEATH 1-12 KILDARE 1-10

THIS SECOND REPLAY came nowhere near matching the near classic quality of the second drawn game. Fair to say, it also fell some distance short of the first encounter. Perhaps it was asking too much to expect the Meath and Kildare players to deliver another showpiece so soon after running themselves to a standstill two weeks earlier. Two hundred and forty minutes of total commitment, bone-crushing, die-for-the-next-ball endeavour between the two same teams is bound to take its toll.

No one should be too surprised that a third Championship meeting in a month between neighbouring rivals Meath and Kildare failed to produce a classic. It was never likely to be one. Greasy underfoot conditions hardly helped matters and the pressure and intensity of the occasion seemed to get to some of the players. There was an air of tension throughout the game, in stark contrast to the atmosphere of the two drawn encounters. Four players were sent-off while six more were booked by Longford referee Pat O'Toole.

Meath won much more possession around the midfield area on this occasion and that was a major factor in the final analysis. And then there was Ollie Murphy. The Carnaross player had the game of his life in a Meath jersey and emerged as top scorer with 1-4, all from play. Vintage. A fortnight earlier, Jody Devine saved Meath from certain defeat; this time, Ollie Murphy proved to be their trump card.

Unlike their two previous meetings in this year's Championship, Kildare had to fight an uphill battle from the very start as Meath took control from the outset. Full-forward Brendan Reilly was very much to the fore early on and the Dunboyne flyer tacked on two points to John McDermott's opener to leave the All-Ireland champions three points clear after eleven minutes play.

Kildare were dealt a hammer blow after just sixteen minutes when Davy Dalton was sent-off after he collided with Brendan Reilly. The Kildare full-back immediately called for attention as Reilly lay on the ground suffering from concussion. Dalton was devastated to be sent-off and subsequently protested his innocence.

Ollie Murphy's third point in the 23rd minute put the All-Ireland champions 0-7 to 0-1 ahead and seemingly cruising. Kildare displayed tremendous character at this juncture and Padraig Graven settled their nerves when he landed his second pointed free. Niall Buckley converted a 45' as Kildare clawed their way back into the game. Then, Meath's Mark O'Reilly and Kildare's Brian Murphy were both sent off for a second bookable offence. Niall Buckley once again found the target from a '45 and Martin Lynch scored a point before Meath replied with a point each from Trevor Giles and Jimmy McGuinness. Half-time score: Meath 0-9 Kildare 0-5.

Kildare were presented with a golden opportunity shortly after the re-start when

Padraig Graven was fouled by Darren Fay and the referee awarded a penalty. Eddie McCormack took on the responsibility but struck the ball over the bar. Graven and the in-form Tommy Dowd exchanged points before Fay received his marching orders for an off-the-ball foul on Martin Lynch. Soon afterwards, Ollie Murphy struck for a goal to stretch Meath's advantage to six points but Kildare came storming back and a goal from Declan Kerrigan ensured no one was in any hurry to exit Croke Park. The impressive Buckley rowed in with two more pointed frees to reduce the deficit to a single point. But the equalising point failed to materialise and 'Man Of The Match', Ollie Murphy, crowned a magnificent display with the final point of the afternoon. Meath still alive; still Leinster and All-Ireland Champions, but Offaly are waiting patiently in the wings. Beware!

SCORERS - MEATH: Ollie Murphy 1-4; Brendan Reilly 0-2, Trevor Giles 0-2; John McDermott 0-1; Tommy Dowd 0-1; Jimmy McGuinness 0-1; Colm Coyle 0-1
KILDARE: Niall Buckley 0-5; Padraig Graven 0-3; Declan Kerrigan 1-0;
Eddie McCormack 0-1; Martin Lynch 0-1

MEATH

Conor Martin

Mark O'Reilly — Darren Fay — Martin O'Connell

Paddy Reynolds — Enda McManus — Donal Curtis

Jimmy McGuinness — John McDermott

Trevor Giles — Tommy Dowd — Nigel Nestor

Colm Coyle — Brendan Reilly — Ollie Murphy

SUBSTITUTES: P.J. Gillic for Brendan Reilly; Jody Devine for P.J. Gillic

KILDARE

Christy Byrne

Martin Ryan — Davy Dalton — Sos Dowling

Anthony Rainbow — Glen Ryan — Ken Doyle

Niall Buckley — Willie McCreery

Eddie McCormack — Declan Kerrigan — Tom Harris

Padraig Graven — Martin Lynch — Brian Murphy

SUBSTITUTES: John Finn for Tom Harris; Paul McCormack for Padraig Graven

MEATH
BACK ROW L TO R: Trevor Giles, John McDermott, Jimmy McGuinness, Martin O'Connell, Brendan Reilly, Tommy Dowd, Nigel Nestor;
FRONT ROW L TO R: Colm Coyle, Mark O'Reilly, Donal Curtis, Ollie Murphy, Conor Martin, Darren Fay, Paddy Reynolds, Enda McManus.

SATURDAY, AUGUST 16, 1997

LEINSTER SENIOR FOOTBALL CHAMPIONSHIP FINAL

OFFALY versus MEATH

CROKE PARK

REFEREE: BRIAN WHITE (WEXFORD)

RESULT: OFFALY 3-17 MEATH 1-15

TOMMY LYONS had a dream a few nights before the game that Offaly would beat Meath by seven points. Reality was even better. Offaly regained the Leinster crown after a gap of fifteen years by no less than eight points. An astonishing result. It was necessary to look at the scoreboard more than once at the end of the game just to confirm that our eyes were not deceiving us.

Coming into the Leinster Final, Offaly had won fifteen, drawn one and lost just one of their eighteen games under the guidance of Tommy Lyons. An incredible record! However, few outside the confines of their own county gave Offaly even a remote chance of beating the All-Ireland Champions, but Lyons never wavered in his belief that his players had the ability to shock Meath. But not even in his wildest dreams, could the Mayo-born manager have envisaged his team winning with such conviction and confidence. Super-fit Offaly took the game to their more illustrious opponents right from the throw-in and continued to grow in confidence as the game progressed. Meath looked jaded at times, but typically Seán Boylan's men gave their all like true champions. Meath were forced to line-out without four key players and their absence was evident from very early on. Mark O'Reilly, Darren Fay, Martin O'Connell and Graham Geraghty were sorely missed, but nothing should ever be allowed detract from Offaly's magnificent performance. It represented everything positive and enriching in Gaelic Football. The perfect advertisement for a wonderful game.

Vinny Claffey, Roy Malone and Peter Brady accounted for 3-8 of Offaly's total and continually exposed the Meath full-back line. Other notable features: Offaly scored 3-15 from play and had established a ten points lead, 2-6 to 0-2, by the 21st minute. Offaly wing-forward David Reynolds scored the opening point of the game, but very soon afterwards Meath were swarming forward in search of scores. However, the champions missed four eminently scorable chances much to dismay of their supporters.

Roy Malone scored the first goal of the game after nine minutes play and even at that early stage it was obvious that the All-Ireland Champions were struggling. Their problems were further exacerbated when Vinny Claffey scored Offaly's second goal midway through the first-half after good work by Seán Grennan.

Brendan Reilly, easily Meath's best player, turned the tide in favour of the champions with some good scores and the margin was down to a more manageable five points at the interval, Offaly 2-6, Meath 0-7. Furthermore, Offaly goalkeeper Padraig Kelly denied Reilly a certain goal with a superb save, while a Jimmy McGuinness shot hit the butt of the upright and went wide.

Trevor Giles and McGuinness, impressive throughout, scored a point each early in the second-half, but Claffey replied with two well-taken points. Giles, Reilly and McGuinness were keeping Meath afloat as Offaly fought desperately to preserve their lead. Then came the crucial score! Lightning-fast Roy Malone raced through the Meath defence at breakneck speed and let fly for a spectacular goal that turned the game decisively in Offaly's favour.

Somehow Meath rallied again and McGuinness reduced the margin to four points with a well-taken goal. Could Meath pull it off? Vinny Claffey answered that question in emphatic style when he fired over two points in quick succession. Offaly finished with a flourish and a point apiece from Colm Quinn and 'Man Of The Match' Claffey ensured Tommy Lyons' dream, and the dreams of ever Offaly player and supporter, had come true.

SCORERS - OFFALY: Vinny Claffey 1-5; Roy Malone 2-0; Colm Quinn 0-4; Peter Brady 0-3; David Reynolds 0-3; Ronan Mooney 0-1; Ciaran McManus 0-1
MEATH: Brendan Reilly 0-7; Jimmy McGuinness 1-2; Trevor Giles 0-3; Ollie Murphy 0-3

OFFALY

Padraig Kelly

Cathal Daly — Larry Carroll — Barry Malone

John Kenny — Finbar Cullen — Tom Coffey

Ciaran McManus — Ronan Mooney

Colm Quinn — Sean Grennan — David Reynolds

Vinny Claffey — Roy Malone — Peter Brady

SUBSTITUTES: Phil O'Reilly for Larry Carroll; James Grennan for David Reynolds

MEATH

Conor Martin

Donal Curtis — Enda McManus — Ned Kearney

Nigel Nestor — Kevin Cahill — Paddy Reynolds

Jimmy McGuinness — John McDermott

Trevor Giles — Tommy Dowd — P.J. Gillic

Colm Coyle — Brendan Reilly — Ollie Murphy

SUBSTITUTES: Jody Devine for Colm Coyle; Evan Kelly for P.J. Gillic

OFFALY
BACK ROW L TO R: Larry Carroll, John Kenny, Barry Malone, Seán Grennan, Colm Quinn, Peter Brady, Roy Malone, Ciaran McManus;
FRONT ROW L TO R: Cathal Daly, David Reynolds, Tom Coffey, Finbar Cullen, Ronan Mooney, Vinny Claffey, Padraig Kelly.

MEATH
BACK ROW L TO R: Trevor Giles, John McDermott, Jimmy McGuinness, Tommy Dowd, P.J. Gillic, Brendan Reilly, Kevin Cahill, Nigel Nestor;
FRONT ROW L TO R: Colm Coyle, Donal Curtis, Ollie Murphy, Ned Kearney, Conor Martin, Paddy Reynolds, Enda McManus.

SUNDAY, MAY 18, 1997

ULSTER SENIOR FOOTBALL CHAMPIONSHIP PRELIMINARY ROUND

TYRONE versus DOWN

ST. TIGHEARNACH'S PARK, CLONES

REFEREE: MICHAEL MCGRATH, DONEGAL

RESULT: TYRONE 0-15 DOWN 2-9 (A DRAW)

DEFENDING CHAMPIONS TYRONE were under no illusions about the enormity of their task in this preliminary round tie against a Down team determined to make amends for their defeat in last year's provincial decider. Both teams had much to prove! Tyrone had suffered a heavy defeat against Meath in last year's All-Ireland semi-final, while Down had played well below par against Kerry in the League quarter-final in April losing by eleven points. No one was quite sure what to expect in Clones!

Tyrone were on the brink of defeat until Adrian Cush levelled the game with a close-range free with four minutes remaining after Down keeper, Mickey McVeigh, was penalised. Afterwards, Down manager Peter McGrath expressed himself unhappy with some of referee Michael McGrath's decisions during the course of the game.

Down were reduced to fourteen players after 46 minutes when Peter Withnell received his marching orders after committing a second bookable offence. Earlier, Withnell had his name taken after the lineman reported him for an off-the-ball foul on a Tyrone defender.

Only 12,572 attended the game which was littered with mistakes but embellished by many fine individual performances. The match finished in a welter of excitement as Tyrone fought tenaciously for Championship survival and were glad to get a reprieve.

The first half was no more than mediocre! Adrian Cush and Peter Canavan were prominent early on as Tyrone built up a 0-6 to 0-3 lead after 23 minutes. John 'Shorty' Treanor accounted for those three Down points with solid free taking. Gerard Cavlan and Jody Gormley held the upperhand at midfield in that period of Tyrone dominance. But just when it appeared the Ulster Champions would consolidate their position, Down were awarded a penalty which was converted in impressive style by Gary Mason to level the game. Conor Deegan was now beginning to make an impact at midfield, but the giant midfielder missed a great chance of a goal when he drove the ball narrowly wide as the first half neared a finish.

However, Conor's brother, Gerard, struck a powerful shot to the roof of the Tyrone net after 55 minutes to put fourteen-man Down four points ahead, 2-8 to 0-10. The goal was allowed even though Deegan appeared to take more than the requisite number of steps before despatching the ball past Finbar McConnell.

At the other end, Mickey McVeigh deprived Tyrone substitute Brian Dooher a certain goal with a superb diving save. Dooher, more than any other player, was instrumental in Tyrone's revival. All-Star Peter Canavan pointed a free; Adrian Cush tacked on two more before Dooher landed the equalising point after 62 minutes.

'Shorty' Treanor pointed a long-range free to put the Down supporters in a celebratory mood before Cush converted a thirteen metres free to ensure Tyrone survived to fight another day. But only just!

SCORERS - TYRONE: Adrian Cush 0-6; Peter Canavan 0-4; Stephen Lawn 0-2; Ciaran McBride 0-1; Brian Dooher 0-1; Noel Donnelly 0-1
DOWN: John 'Shorty' Treanor 0-5; Gary Mason 1-1; Gerard Deegan 1-1; Mickey Linden 0-2

TYRONE

Finbar McConnell

Paul Devlin — Paul O'Neill — Chris Lawn

Noel Donnelly — Fergal Logan — Paul Donnelly

Jody Gormley — Gerard Cavlan

Adrian Cush — Seamus McCallan — Ciaran Loughran

Ciaran McBride — Stephen Lawn — Peter Canavan

SUBSTITUTES: Brian Dooher for Gerard Cavlan; Fay Devlin for Chris Lawn

DOWN

Mickey McVeigh

Gary Mason — Sean Ward — Liam Howlett

Daniel Flynn — Ross Carr — Cathal Murray

Conor Deegan — Gregory McCartan

John 'Shorty' Treanor — Greg Blaney — Peter Withnell

Mickey Linden — Ciaran McCabe — Gerard Deegan

SUBSTITUTES: James McCartan for Ciaran McCabe; Aidan Farrell for Greg Blaney

TYRONE
BACK ROW L TO R: Paul Devlin, Jody Gormley, Adrian Cush, Joe Cassidy, Mattie McGleenan, Seamus McCallan, Finbar McConnell, Paul O'Neill, Fergal Logan, Gerard Cavlan, Aidan Morris, Ciaran McBride;
FRONT ROW L TO R: Brian McGuckian, Eoin Gormley, Brian Dooher, Ronan McGarrity, Benny Owens, Stephen Lawn, Noel Donnelly, Peter Canavan, Ciaran Loughran, Chris Lawn, Paul Donnelly, Fay Devlin.

DOWN
BACK ROW L TO R: John 'Shorty' Treanor, Conor Deegan, Ciaran McCabe, Seán Ward, Mickey McVeigh, Mickey Linden, Greg Blaney, Peter Withnell;
FRONT ROW L TO R. Ross Carr, Gerard Deegan, Cathal Murray, Gregory McCartan, Liam Howlett, Gary Mason, Daniel Flynn.

SUNDAY, MAY 25, 1997

ULSTER SENIOR FOOTBALL CHAMPIONSHIP PRELIMINARY ROUND (REPLAY)

TYRONE versus DOWN

ST. TIGHEARNACH'S PARK, CLONES

REFEREE: MICHAEL McGRATH (DONEGAL)

RESULT: TYRONE 3-8 DOWN 1-11

THE TYRONE BANDWAGON rolls on! Adrian Cush rescued the defending champions the previous week in Clones with a late equalising point and the Donaghmore player also made a very considerable contribution in the replay with a tally of five points.

Some 24,622, nearly double the attendance of the previous week, watched on in bright sunshine as Tyrone finally shook off a dogged Down challenge in a compelling encounter that produced no less than four goals.

Down hauled back a four points half-time deficit to move two points clear near the midway point of the second-half before goals from Peter Canavan and super-sub, Mattie McGleenan, finally decided the issue in favour of the holders.

Tyrone and Down were both forced to make changes before the start because of injuries to key players, Gerard Cavlan and Greg Blaney. Seán McLoughlin came into the Tyrone side in place of Cavlan, while Aidan Farrell replaced Blaney at centre-half-forward. Fay Devlin lined out at centre-half-back for Tyrone with Fergal Logan moving to midfield alongside Enda Kilpatrick.

Down goalkeeper Mickey McVeigh brought off a magnificent save to deny Ciaran McBride a goal after just four minutes play. The match was on in earnest but scores were in limited supply. The sides were level 0-2 apiece when Peter Canavan gathered a long pass from Enda Kilpatrick before setting up full-forward Stephen Lawn for the first goal of the game.

The Tyrone defence never allowed the Down forwards settle on the ball; Kilpatrick was outstanding at midfield in the first half while Cush and Canavan provided leadership in attack. Both sides squandered scoring chances but Tyrone were happiest with their lot at the interval after establishing a 1-5 to 0-4 lead.

But Down were soon back on level terms! Conor Deegan scored a point from play and the same player combined in a move which set up Ciaran McCabe for a goal which levelled the game for the third time, little more than five minutes after the re-start.

Mickey Linden and substitute Finbar Caulfield scored a point each to deservedly push Down two points clear, before Canavan and McGleenan made their mark. Firstly, McGleenan floated a high ball into the Down goal area where Ciaran McBride challenged goalkeeper Mickey McVeigh and the ever-dangerous Canavan dived to fist the loose ball to the net.

Linden and Cush then exchanged points before McGleenan flicked a Canavan free over the head of goalkeeper McVeigh for the decisive score of the game.

Down continued to press hard in the closing stages to regain the initiative, but champions Tyrone weathered the storm and eventually prevailed by a three points margin.

TYRONE - SCORERS: Adrian Cush 0-5; Peter Canavan 1-1; Stephen Lawn 1-0; Mattie McGleenan 1-0; Enda Kilpatrick 0-1; Seamus McCallan 0-1
SCORERS: John 'Shorty' Treanor 0-4; Ciaran McCabe 1-1; Mickey Linden 0-3; Conor Deegan 0-1; Gerard Deegan 0-1; Finbar McCaulfield 0-1

TYRONE

Finbar McConnell

Paul Devlin — Paul O'Neill — Chris Lawn
Noel Donnelly — Fay Devlin — Sean McLoughlin

Fergal Logan — Enda Kilpatrick

Adrian Cush — Seamus McCallan — Ciaran Loughran
Ciaran McBride — Stephen Lawn — Peter Canavan

SUBSTITUTES: Brian Dooher for Ciaran Loughran; Mattie McGleenan for Fergal Logan; Jody Gormley for Enda Kilpatrick

DOWN

Mickey McVeigh

Gary Mason — Sean Ward — Liam Howlett
Daniel Flynn — Ross Carr — Cathal Murray

Conor Deegan — Gregory McCartan

John 'Shorty' Treanor — Aidan Farrell — James McCartan
Mickey Linden — Ciaran McCabe — Gerard Deegan

SUBSTITUTES: Finbar Caulfield for Daniel Flynn; Simon Poland for Seán Ward

SUNDAY, MAY 25, 1997

ULSTER SENIOR FOOTBALL CHAMPIONSHIP

DONEGAL versus ANTRIM

MAC CUMHAILL PARK, BALLYBOFEY

REFEREE: BRENDAN GORMAN (ARMAGH)

RESULT: DONEGAL 2-12 ANTRIM 1-13

DONEGAL CAME PERILOUSLY close to being dumped out of the Championship by a fiercely committed and totally focused Antrim team determined to cast aside the tag of no-hopers.

Donegal appeared to be coasting to victory when they led by no less than nine points entering the final quarter, but a brave Antrim side rallied strongly in the closing stages and were unlucky not to gain at least a draw. Put simply: Donegal players felt their work for the day was complete after establishing a big lead, while a revitalised Antrim persevered to the very end and narrowly failed to pull off a shock victory.

It was a dramatic turnaround which began in earnest when impressive Antrim substitute, Kevin Madden, scored a superb goal to reduce the margin to just three points. The goal was the culmination of a period of Antrim dominance which had yielded three points - two from Paul Derby and one from Madden.

Donegal were now in an extremely vulnerable position but Brian McLoughlin showed good composure to land a fine point from play to steer his side clear of the danger zone. But there was more trauma to endure for Donegal players and supporters before victory was claimed. Jimmy Wilson scored a point for Antrim before an all-out onslaught almost resulted in the equalising goal. Defenders Aidan Short and Martin Mulholland threw caution to the wind in a last-ditch attempt to save the game. Short soloed through a tiring Donegal defence before delivering a pass to the in-rushing Mulholland whose intentions were absolutely clear to everyone. However, the full-back could only watch in despair as his goal-bound shot whistled over the crossbar much to the relief of the large home support.

That frenetic finish was a far cry from the early stages of the game which saw Donegal race into a commanding 1-4 to 0-1 lead by the midway point of the first half with the goal coming from Tony Boyle. But a highly motivated Antrim team eventually began to make good use of quality possession and had drawn within three points of their more fancied opponents by the half-time interval.

It looked bleak for Antrim shortly after the re-start when Donegal midfielder Brian Murray fisted a goal after a long pass from Barry McGowan. Donegal continued to dominate proceedings and had stretched their lead to nine points and appeared to be coasting to victory when Antrim began the fightback which resulted in a grandstand finish.

SCORERS - DONEGAL: Manus Boyle 0-4; Brian Murray 1-1; Tony Boyle 1-0; Declan Bonner 0-2; Jim McGuinness 0-1; Barry McGowan 0-1; Noel Hegarty 0-1; Brian McLoughlin 0-1; Adrian Sweeney 0-1
ANTRIM: Kevin Madden 1-1; Frank Wilson 0-3; Paul Derby 0-3; Jimmy Wilson 0-2;
Peter McCann 0-2; David Smyth 0-1; Martin Mulholland 0-1

DONEGAL

	Paul Callaghan	
Matt Gallagher	John Joe Doherty	John Cunningham
Barry McGowan	Mark Crossan	Sean McEwen
James Ruane		Brian Murray
Jim McGuinness	Noel Hegarty	Adrian Sweeney
Declan Bonner	Tony Boyle	Manus Boyle

SUBSTITUTES: Peter McGinley for Matt Gallagher; Brian McLoughlin for Adrian Sweeney

ANTRIM

	Sean McGreevy	
Gerard McCarren	Martin Mulholland	Locky McCurdy
Donal Armstrong	Aiden Short	John Kelly
Chris Murphy		Paul Erlean
Frank Wilson	Jimmy Wilson	Colum McCabe
Paul Derby	Frank Fitzsimons	David Smyth

SUBSTITUTES: Peter McCann for Donal Armstrong;
Kevin Madden for Colum McCabe; Mickey Boyle for Chris Murphy

SUNDAY, JUNE 1, 1997

ULSTER SENIOR FOOTBALL CHAMPIONSHIP QUARTER-FINAL

DERRY versus MONAGHAN

ST. TIGHEARNACH'S PARK, CLONES

REFEREE: MARTIN McBRIEN (FERMANAGH)

RESULT: DERRY 1-11 MONAGHAN 2-8 (A DRAW)

MONAGHAN CAME CLOSE to causing a major upset against favourites Derry in what was poor quality fare at Clones before an attendance of over ten thousand. Fermanagh referee Martin McBrien awarded well over eighty frees in a game which saw Monaghan's Joe Coyle and Derry's Brian McCormack dismissed for an off-the-ball incident in the early stages of the second-half. But despite the sendings off and the large number of frees, it was by no means a malicious game. Joe Brolly and Joe Cassidy were perhaps the only Derry players to enhance their reputations while Peter Duffy turned in a 'Man of the Match' performance for Monaghan.

Derry were given a reprieve as early as the second minute when a Peter Duffy penalty hit the post and rebounded to safety. That let-off failed to lift Derry and instead it was Monaghan who applied the pressure with telling effect. Favoured by the breeze, Monaghan's policy of bombarding a less-than-assured Derry defence with one high ball after another paid handsome dividends in the opening half. Duffy atoned for his penalty miss by scoring a superb goal after eighteen minutes to push Monaghan 1-3 to 0-3 ahead. The lightning-fast Castleblayney player bounded past the Derry defence and crashed the ball to the net. Earlier, McGinnity had proved his pedigree as a free-taker by landing three points, and the same player converted another free to further dishearten the opposition.

To make matters worse for Derry, Monaghan corner-back Noel Marron gratefully collected a breaking ball and beat goalkeeper Damien McCusker. Marron's goal left Monaghan seven points clear and in the driving seat. But Derry halted the slide and two points apiece from key forwards, Joe Brolly and Joe Cassidy, reduced the margin to a much more respectable three points by the half-time break.

Derry maintained the momentum after the re-start: Cassidy pointed a free before Brolly once again underlined his class as a goal scorer. The speedy Dungiven man got inside the Monaghan defence and deftly placed the ball wide of goalkeeper Glenn Murphy for a well-executed goal. Truly, a Brolly special and celebrated in typically flamboyant style.

Although Brolly tacked on a point from a free, it soon became evident that Monaghan had no intention of capitulating. Derry, too, were having problems of their own and were clearly unable to shake off a dogged Monaghan challenge. Both teams were reduced to fourteen players when Brian McCormack and Joe Coyle were ordered to the line.

With Duffy tormenting the Derry defence, Monaghan had fought back to level terms as the game entered the third quarter.

Anthony Tohill and Stephen McGinnity exchanged points before Joe Cassidy edged Derry ahead once again with a fine point. But in the end, justice was done when corner-forward Declan McKieran scored the equalising point from a free. Emmet McKeever was booked near the finish for a foul on Peter Duffy, but instead of awarding a free to Monaghan, the referee decided to throw in the ball after adjudging that Gregory Flanagan had retaliated.

SCORERS - DERRY: Joe Brolly 1-4; Joe Cassidy 0-5; Anthony Tohill 0-2
MONAGHAN: Stephen McGinnity 0-5; Peter Duffy 1-1; Noel Marron 1-0;
Declan McKiernan 0-1; Dermot McArdle 0-1

DERRY

Damien McCusker

Kieran McKeever — David O'Neill — Emmett McKeever

Karl Diamond — Henry Downey — Johnny McBride

Anthony Tohill — Dermot Dougan

Fergal McCusker — Brian McCormack — Joe Cassidy

Joe Brolly — Dermot Heaney — Ronan Rocks

SUBSTITUTES: Adrian McGuckian for Ronan Rocks;
Enda Muldoon for Fergal McCusker; Gary Coleman for Emmett McKeever

MONAGHAN

Glen Murphy

Edwin Murphy — Dermot Duffy — Noel Marron

Joe Coyle — Gerard McGurk — John Conlon

Frank McEnaney — Padraig McShane

Peter Duffy — Mark Daly — Dermot McArdle

Stephen McGinnity — Gregory Flanagan — Declan McKiernan

SUBSTITUTES: Aidan Tavey for Padraig McShane; Colin McCaul for Aidan Tavey; Padraig McDonald for Dermot McArdle

DERRY
BACK ROW L TO R: Brian McCormack, Anthony Tohill, Damien McCusker, Dermot Dougan, Dermot Heaney, Karl Diamond, Ronan Rocks;
FRONT ROW L TO R: Henry Downey, Fergal McCusker, Kieran McKeever, Emmett McKeever, Johnny McBride, David O'Neill, Joe Cassidy. (Missing Joe Brolly)

MONAGHAN
BACK ROW L TO R: Cyril Ronaghan, Colin McAree, Dermot Duffy, Peter Duffy, Gerard McGurk, Glen Murphy, Joe Coyle, Colin McCaul, John Conlon, Mark Daly, Padraig McShane;
MIDDLE ROW L TO R: Edwin Murphy, Noel Marron, Declan McKernan, Frank McEnaney, Dermot McArdle, Stephen McGinnity, Gregory Flanagan, Pauric McDonald, Michael Thompson, Declan Loughman;
FRONT ROW (seated) L TO R: Aidan Tavey, Vincent Martin, Brian Morgan.

SUNDAY, JUNE 8, 1997

ULSTER SENIOR FOOTBALL CHAMPIONSHIP QUARTER-FINAL (REPLAY)

DERRY versus MONAGHAN

CELTIC PARK

REFEREE: MARTIN McBRIEN (FERMANAGH)

RESULT: DERRY 2-15 MONAGHAN 0-10

ALTHOUGH DERRY POWERED their way to a comprehensive eleven points victory over Monaghan, clearly the Oak Leaf county are still some way short of the finished article. It must be remembered that Monaghan were forced to play more than sixty minutes with just fourteen players after Stephen McGinnity received his marching orders early in the first-half for an off-the-ball foul on Derry wing-back Johnny McBride. McGinnity was clearly annoyed at being sent-off and he made his displeasure known to McBride as he left the field. It was the worst possible scenario for a young team against the more experienced red and white Derry machine, playing in their own back yard.

Monaghan were a trifle unlucky not to gain the verdict in the drawn game, but the loss of McGinnity after just eight minutes ensured that Derry held the upperhand throughout this replayed encounter. Monaghan came into the game brimming with confidence after their gutsy display the previous Sunday, but McGinnity's dismissal and a goal for Derry centre-half-forward Dermot Dougan soon afterwards made their task well-nigh impossible.

Joe Brolly's initial point attempt rebounded off the post and Dougan reacted quickest to finish the ball to the net.

With Dermot Heaney on top of his game at midfield and Henry Downey and Kieran McKeever ably marshalling the defence, Derry stamped their authority on the game. Brolly and Seamus Downey tormented the Monaghan defence and were the dominant forwards as Derry coasted into a commanding 2-7 to 0-4 half-time lead. All-Star Brolly scored Derry's second goal approaching half-time when Dougan returned the compliment with a good pass and the Dungiven 'smiler' steered the ball past Glenn Murphy for a splendid goal. And then off he roamed on his familiar routine, blowing kisses to the Derry faithful. Gaelic football is richer because of charismatic players like Joe Brolly!

Fourteen-man Monaghan hardly deserved to be nine points in arrears at the interval after winning a lot of quality possession and being deprived a goal when a Mark Daly flicked effort struck the woodwork.

Declan Smyth was introduced just before half-time and he added sparkle to the Monaghan forward line. Smyth converted a thirteen-metres free shortly after the re-start and that was followed by a point from Noel Marron to reduce the margin to seven points. It was the closest Monaghan came to Derry for the remainder of the game. The highly-impressive Seán Martin Lockhart, who came on in place of Karl Diamond at half-time, used his speed to great effect as Monaghan came under even more intense pressure. Gary Coleman was also superb in the Derry defence. Here surely is one of the most talented and athletic defenders in gaelic football! Anthony Tohill showed flashes of the brilliance that marks him out as a player of special talent!

Dermot Heaney had a goal disallowed as rampant Derry took full advantage of their extra player. Substitute Declan Smyth scored four points for Monaghan in the second-half, but all round Derry had far too much power and mobility and in the end fashioned an emphatic victory.

SCORERS - DERRY: Joe Brolly 1-4; Seamus Downey 0-3; Dermot Dougan 1-0; Fergal McCusker 0-2; Joe Cassidy 0-2; Ronan Rocks 0-1; Dermot Heaney 0-1; Sean Martin Lockhart 0-1; Kieran McKeever 0-1
MONAGHAN: Declan Smyth 0-5; Declan McKiernan 0-2; Noel Marron 0-2; Peter Duffy 0-1

DERRY

Damien McCusker

Kieran McKeever — David O'Neill — Gary Coleman

Karl Diamond — Henry Downey — Johnny McBride

Anthony Tohill — Dermot Heaney

Gary Magill — Dermot Dougan — Fergal McCusker

Joe Brolly — Seamus Downey — Joe Cassidy

SUBSTITUTES: Seán Martin Lockhart for Karl Diamond;
Enda Muldoon for Gary McGill; Ronan Rocks for Seamus Downey

MONAGHAN

Glen Murphy

Dermot McArdle — Gerard McGurk — Dermot Duffy

Noel Marron — Edwin Murphy — John Conlon

Frank McEnaney — Colm McCaul

Stephen McGinnity — Mark Daly — Peter Duffy

Gregory Flanagan — Declan Loughman — Declan McKiernan

SUBSTITUTES: Declan Smyth for Declan Loughman;
Padraig McShane for Declan McKiernan; Vincent Martin for Mark Daly

SUNDAY, JUNE 8, 1997

ULSTER SENIOR FOOTBALL CHAMPIONSHIP QUARTER-FINAL

CAVAN versus FERMANAGH

ST. TIGHEARNACH'S PARK, CLONES

REFEREE: JIM CURRAN (TYRONE)

RESULT: CAVAN 1-12 FERMANAGH 1-12 (A DRAW)

SUBSTITUTE ANTHONY FORDE was the toast of the large Cavan contingent at Clones when he landed an equalising point almost five minutes into injury-time to deprive Fermanagh of a rare Championship victory. Outsiders Fermanagh, the only county never to win the Ulster Senior Football Championship title, showed a marked improvement on last year's dismal form against Tyrone and were somewhat unlucky not to savour a long-awaited slice of Championship glory.

When corner-forward Mickey Graham sent over a point to stretch Cavan's lead to three points with less than four minutes remaining, Fermanagh's cause appeared lost. But the drama was only beginning!

The All-Ireland 'B' Champions displayed tremendous battling qualities and the game came to life when their star player, Raymond Gallagher, scored a truly magnificent goal to level scores at 1-10 each. Few goals in any Championship year would compare to Gallagher's high quality piledriver after incisive approach work from Collie Curran and Paul Brewster. I have watched the goal many times since on video and still marvel at the quality of Gallagher's clinical left-footed finish. Make no mistake, Gallagher is unquestionably one of the finest forwards in present day gaelic football. A player of exceptional talent!

That goal from Gallagher sparked a Fermanagh revival that had fourteen-man Cavan fighting tooth-and-nail for their Championship survival. Cavan had been reduced in number ten minutes before half-time when defender Philip Kermath was ordered off for a second bookable offence, but despite that setback, the men from Breffni played good possession football and always looked likely winners until Gallagher gave Fermanagh a lifeline.

Peter Reilly edged Cavan ahead with normal time almost up, but Liam McBarron equalised in injury-time and Gallagher looked to have sealed victory for Fermanagh when he fired over the lead point from play. McBarron had a great chance to seal victory but shot wide from a very scorable position and soon after Forde fired over the equalising point to force a replay.

Dermot McCabe scored the Cavan goal in the opening half when he got in behind the Fermanagh defence and fisted a Peter Reilly free over the head of Fermanagh goalkeeper, Cormac McAdam.

Cavan held a two points advantage at the interval, 1-5 to 0-6, and Jason Reilly came close to extending that lead shortly after the re-start, but he missed two goal chances in quick succession.

In an evenly balanced second-half, Cavan just held the edge until Gallagher's goal rocked them back on their heels and sent shock waves through their football-mad supporters.

Cavan wasted a lot of scoring chances throughout the game and, as the finish approached, it appeared they would pay a heavy price for their waywardness. Fermanagh, too, failed to convert all the chances that came their way but no one could fault their brilliant forward, Raymond Gallagher, who ended the game with a personal tally of 1-7. Surely a 'Man of the Match' performance!

SCORERS - CAVAN: Peter Reilly 0-5; Dermot McCabe 1-1;
Raymond Cunningham 0-3; Mickey Graham 0-2; Anthony Forde 0-1
FERMANAGH: Raymond Gallagher 1-7; Liam McBarron 0-2; Shane King 0-1; Colin Curran 0-1;
Kieran Donnelly 0-1

CAVAN

Paul O'Dowd

Philip Kermath | Ciaran Brady | Damien O'Reilly

Gerry Sheridan | Bernard Morris | Patrick Sheils

Stephen King | Philip Smith

Dermot McCabe | Peter Reilly | Raymond Cunningham

Jason Reilly | Fintan Cahill | Mickey Graham

SUBSTITUTES: Larry Reilly for Jason Reilly;
Anthony Forde for Philip Smith; Ronan Carolan for Larry Reilly

FERMANAGH

Cormac McAdam

Rory McEnhill | Seán Breen | Paddy McGuinness

Tommy Callaghan | Barry King | Justin Gilheany

Paul Brewster | Colm Courtney

Raymond Johnson | Colin Curran | Kieran Donnelly

Raymond Gallagher | Liam McBarron | Shane King

SUBSTITUTES: Raymond Curran for Justin Gilheany;
Mark Gallagher for Raymond Johnson

CAVAN

BACK ROW L TO R: Peter Reilly, Dermot McCabe, Patrick Sheils, Paul O'Dowd, Damien O'Reilly, Bernard Morris; FRONT ROW L TO R: Ciaran Brady, Gerry Sheridan, Philip Smith, Jason Reilly, Stephen King, Mickey Graham, Fintan Cahill, Raymond Cunningham, Philip Kermath.

FERMANAGH
BACK ROW L TO R: Rory McEnhill, Liam McBarron, Paul Brewster, Colm Courtney, Seán Breen, Paddy McGuinness, Justin Gilheany, Barry King, Colin Curran;
FRONT ROW L TO R: Tommy Callaghan, Cormac McAdam, Shane King, Raymond Gallagher, Kieran Donnelly, Raymond Johnson.

SUNDAY, JUNE 15, 1997

ULSTER SENIOR FOOTBALL CHAMPIONSHIP QUARTER-FINAL (REPLAY)

CAVAN versus FERMANAGH

ST. TIGHEARNACH'S PARK, CLONES

REFEREE: JIM CURRAN (TYRONE)

RESULT: CAVAN 0-14 FERMANAGH 0-11

CAVAN WERE FORTUNATE to escape with a draw the previous week when Anthony Forde scored an equalising point in injury-time to give his side a reprieve. Cavan were reduced to fourteen players in the drawn game when corner-back Philip Kermath was ordered off before the break, but this time it was Fermanagh who suffered the loss of a defender just approaching the interval. Seán Breen was dismissed by referee Jim Curran for a second bookable offence. The Fermanagh full-back was none too happy with the referee's decision which ultimately changed the course of the game.

Breen's dismissal was a huge setback and his loss was particularly evident in the closing stages when Cavan's extra player proved too much for a young and inexperienced Fermanagh side that simply ran out of steam. Pat King's brave fourteen-man team had used up every ounce of energy in search of glory and Cavan only began to reel off the vital scores when Fermanagh tired visibly in the closing ten minutes.

Cavan were under intense pressure from the start against an energetic and fiercely determined Fermanagh side inspired by their midfielder Paul Brewster. Although playing some marvellous attacking football, Fermanagh were only level, 0-2 each, after fifteen minutes play. Stephen Maguire missed a great chance of a goal for Fermanagh when his shot was brilliantly saved by Cavan goalkeeper Paul O'Dowd.

With a two points contribution from Fintan Cahill, Cavan had moved 0-6 to 0-3 ahead at the end of normal time in the first-half. The supply of ball to the Fermanagh forward line was now very sparse and Terry Farrelly, who had replaced Paul Brady after 26 minutes, was making a telling contribution in what up to then was a less than assured Cavan defence.

Two pointed frees in injury-time from Shane King and Raymond Gallagher left fourteen-man Fermanagh trailing by just one point at the interval, but with Breen out of bounds, it was always going to be an uphill battle for the All-Ireland 'B' Champions in the second-half.

Two points for Fermanagh by Shane King in reply to a point from Fintan Cahill brought the sides level early in the second-half. Liam Mc Barron's powerfully struck goal-bound shot rebounded over the crossbar before Fermanagh moved ahead with a point each from Raymond Gallagher and Collie Curran.

Over the next quarter of a hour, Cavan took control and in a purple patch scored seven points without reply against a tiring Fermanagh. It could have been worse for Fermanagh during that period of Cavan dominance only for goalkeeper Cormac McAdam who brought off a superb close-range save from Jason Reilly. Brilliant corner-forward, Mickey Graham was instrumental in Cavan's revival and he turned in an outstanding display. Substitute Ronan Carolan also made a significant impact when introduced to the fray after 54 minutes.

To their credit, Fermanagh never gave up the chase and in a late onslaught Mark and Raymond Gallagher scored a point each to leave just a goal separating the sides at the finish. A close call for Cavan! Fermanagh's day it would appear is not all that far off.

SCORERS- CAVAN: Peter Reilly 0-3; Fintan Cahill 0-3; Mickey Graham 0-2; Dermot McCabe 0-1; Anthony Forde 0-1; Jason Reilly 0-1; Raymond Cunningham 0-1; Ciaran Brady 0-1; Ronan Carolan 0-1
FERMANAGH: Raymond Gallagher 0-5; Shane King 0-3; Collie Curran 0-2; Mark Gallagher 0-1

CAVAN

	Paul O'Dowd	
Damien O'Reilly	Ciaran Brady	Gerry Sheridan
Paul Brady	Bernard Morris	Patrick Sheils
Stephen King		Dermot McCabe
Peter Reilly	Anthony Forde	Raymond Cunningham
Jason Reilly	Fintan Cahill	Mickey Graham

SUBSTITUTES: Terry Farrelly for Paul Brady;
Ronan Carolan for Raymond Cunningham; Larry Reilly for Anthony Forde

FERMANAGH

Cormac McAdam

Mickey Lilly	Sean Breen	Clive Fitzpatrick
Tommy Callaghan	Barry King	Paddy McGuinness
Paul Brewster		Liam McBarron
Raymond Johnston	Colin Curran	Colm Courtney
Raymond Gallagher	Stephen Maguire	Shane King

SUBSTITUTES: Kieran Donnelly for Colm Courtney; Mark Gallagher for Stephen Maguire; Raymond Curran for Mickey Lilly

CAVAN

BACK ROW L TO R: Anthony Forde, Ciaran Brady, Dermot McCabe, Patrick Shiels, Paul O'Dowd, Damien O'Reilly, Bernard Morris, Paul Brady;

FRONT ROW L TO R: Peter Reilly, Mickey Graham, Jason Reilly, Stephen King, Fintan Cahill, Raymond Cunningham, Gerry Sheridan.

FERMANAGH

BACK ROW L TO R: Liam McBarron, Paul Brewster, Stephen Maguire, Colm Courtney, Paddy McGuinness, Seán Breen, Barry King, Colin Curran;

FRONT ROW L TO R: Clive Fitzpatrick, Shane King, Tommy Callaghan, Cormac McAdam, Raymond Gallagher, Raymond Johnston, Mickey Lilly.

SUNDAY, JUNE 15, 1997

ULSTER SENIOR FOOTBALL CHAMPIONSHIP QUARTER-FINAL

TYRONE versus ARMAGH

HEALY PARK, OMAGH

REFEREE: PAT McENANEY (MONAGHAN)

RESULT: TYRONE 1-12 ARMAGH 0-12

SUNDAY JUNE 15 will be remembered above all else as the day young Paul McGirr sadly lost his life while playing for Tyrone minors against Armagh in the Ulster Minor Championship at Omagh.

Seventeen-year-old, Paul, a member of the Dromore club, died in hospital after sustaining injuries in an accidental collision with the Armagh goalkeeper while scoring a crucial goal for his county. It was a tragic death that shocked and saddened everyone.

Tyrone were extremely fortunate to take the honours in this game against a self-destructing Armagh side that shot no fewer than eighteen wides against three for the defending champions.

Put simply, a lack-lustre Tyrone side, outplayed for long periods, had the craft and experience to avail of the limited opportunities that came their way, while Armagh's squandermania cost them a semi-final meeting with Derry. Armagh also failed to take full advantage of their extra player after Tyrone were reduced to fourteen men after 51 minutes when Chris Lawn was sent off by referee Pat McEnaney. Full-back Lawn received his marching orders as a result of a second bookable offence following a foul on wing-forward, Martin Toye. The champions trailed by a point entering the last quarter, but then full-forward Mattie McGleenan turned the game decisively in Tyrone's favour with a controversial goal. McGleenan appeared to push Armagh corner-back Justin McNulty before fisting the ball past Brendan Tierney to edge Tyrone four points clear. It was cruel luck on Armagh who deserved a better result for their unstinting efforts.

Jarlath Burns had an outstanding game at midfield for Armagh and it must have been very frustrating for the brilliant captain to finish on the losing side. However, Armagh failed to capitalise on their midfield dominance and they trailed at half-time by four points, much to the dismay of their supporters. Peter Canavan kept Tyrone in front in the first-half with unerring accuracy from frees. The All-Star scored four points, including one magnificent long-range effort. Tyrone also missed goal chances in the opening half: Canavan had an excellent chance of a goal but his shot was brilliantly saved by Brendan Tierney; McGleenan blasted a close-range effort over the crossbar while Stephen Lawn shot narrowly wide.

Armagh continued their dominance after the interval and restricted Tyrone to just one point in a twenty minute period. Martin Toye and Gerard Cavlan swapped points after the break, but then Armagh took a vice-like grip on the game. It was looking bleak for the Ulster champions when Armagh scored five points without reply to establish a one point lead. Tyrone set about retrieving the situation and Canavan equalised with his fifth free of the match.

Soon afterwards, Adrian Cush suffered an injury and the four-minute delay while he received treatment gave Tyrone the time and space to assess the situation and take remedial action.

Brian Dooher replaced Gerard Cavlan and the U.C.D. student edged Tyrone ahead with a magnificent point from an acute angle. Peter Canavan delivered the pass to Dooher who landed a point off the upright.

One of Tyrone's best players on the day was Mattie McGleenan and it was his late goal which put the game beyond the reach of a gallant but wasteful Armagh team that scarcely deserved to bow out of the Championship.

Armagh free-taker Oisin McConville finished the game as top scorer with a tally of eight points, but it was poor consolation after ending up on the losing side.

SCORERS - TYRONE: Peter Canavan 0-5; Mattie McGleenan 1-2; Adrian Cush 0-2; Gerard Cavlan 0-1; Ciaran McBride 0-1; Brian Dooher 0-1
ARMAGH: Oisin McConville 0-8; Martin Toye 0-1; Ger Houlihan 0-1; Kieran McGeeney 0-1; John Rafferty 0-1

TYRONE

Finbar McConnell

Paul Devlin — Paul O'Neill — Chris Lawn

Noel Donnelly — Fay Devlin — Sean McLoughlin

Enda Kilpatrick — Gerard Cavlan

Adrian Cush — Seamus McCallan — Ciaran McBride

Mattie McGleenan — Stephen Lawn — Peter Canavan

SUBSTITUTES: Jody Gormley for Paul O'Neill; Brian Dooher for Gerard Cavlan

ARMAGH

Brendan Tierney

Enda McNulty — Colm Hanratty — Justin McNulty

John Rafferty — Damien Horisk — Andrew McCann

Jarlath Burns — Kieran McGeeney

Martin Toye — Paul McGrane — Diarmuid Marsden

Ger Houlahan — Neil Smyth — Oisín McConville

SUBSTITUTES: Cathal O'Rourke for Ger Houlahan;
Martin McQuillan for Martin Toye; Cathal Short for Neil Smyth

ARMAGH
BACK ROW L TO R: Colm Hanratty, Neill Smyth, Andrew McCann, Diarmuid Marsden, Ger Houlahan, Paul McGrane, Justin McNulty;
FRONT ROW L TO R: Damien Horisk, Kieran McGeeney, Brendan Tierney, Jarlath Burns, Martin Toye, Oisin McConville, Enda McNulty, John Rafferty

SUNDAY, JUNE 22, 1997

ULSTER SENIOR FOOTBALL CHAMPIONSHIP SEMI-FINAL

CAVAN versus DONEGAL

ST. TIGHEARNACH'S PARK, CLONES

REFEREE: JIM CURRAN (TYRONE)

RESULT: CAVAN 2-16 DONEGAL 2-10

MANAGER MARTIN MCHUGH had mixed emotions after guiding his Cavan team to the Ulster Final at the expense of a Donegal side which contained no less than six of the 1992 All-Ireland winning team of which he himself was a key member. It must have felt strange for McHugh as he patrolled the sideline plotting the downfall of a team that included All-Ireland winning colleagues Brian Murray, John Joe Doherty, Noel Hegarty, Declan Bonner, Tony Boyle and Manus Boyle.

McHugh was centre-half-forward on that historic day in Croke Park in 1992 when Anthony Molloy captained Donegal to their first-ever All-Ireland senior football crown.

Undoubtedly one of the finest footballers of his generation, McHugh had admitted in the week preceding the Ulster semi-final that he was not looking forward to the game, but at the same time emphasised he would do everything in his power to beat Donegal. Hordes of delighted young Cavan supporters converged in the tunnel leading to the dressingrooms after the game clamouring for their newly-crowned hero, McHugh, who has certainly worked the oracle for the 'Breffni Blues' since he took charge as manager.

Cavan deserved their victory on what was a day of triumph for veteran Ronan

Carolan who repaid the manager's faith in him by scoring 1-7 in a match-winning display. Carolan, left out of the starting fifteen in both the draw and replay against Fermanagh, rediscovered his form with a scintillating performance that had Cavan supporters among the attendance of 20,493 singing his praises at the finish.

But this was no one-man show! There was a marked improvement in Cavan's all-round play from their previous outings and the spirit of the team was best exemplified by corner-back Damien O'Reilly, who had to retire with a knee injury midway through the first-half, but returned to the fray late in the game as a forward and provided vital experience in the closing stages. O'Reilly even got his name on the scoresheet with a fisted point to underline his versatility.

Cavan struggled somewhat in the first-half, but Carolan's superb equalising goal four minutes after the restart had a settling effect on the team and the players revelled in the open spaces, as yawning gaps appeared in the Donegal defence.

Peter Reilly's goal at the end of the third quarter was the signal for an all-out onslaught by Cavan and effectively put the game beyond the reach of a struggling Donegal team. Thereafter Cavan played with the confidence of a side in charge of their own destiny as Donegal's challenge faded.

It was a far cry from the early stages of the game when Tony Boyle scored a goal and a point in the opening twelve minutes against a highly porous Cavan defence. There were many anxious faces among the Cavan following in the opening quarter until Ronan Carolan opening their account with a point after sixteen minutes. Carolan's third point of the first-half after 33 minutes brought the sides level 0-6 to 1-3, but two fine points from Manus Boyle left Donegal 1-5 to 0-6 ahead at the interval.

Declan Bonner scored two points for Donegal in the first-half but unfortunately the Na Rossa player had to retire injured in the third quarter and later announced his retirement from inter-county football. Few players have worn the Donegal jersey with such pride and distinction as Bonner and the fact that he lined out in this year's Championship speaks volumes about his bravery after a kidney injury threatened to end his career prematurely.

Donegal lost their shape after Reilly's clinching goal and Cavan marched on to a second Ulster Final in three years.

Cavan played some wonderful direct football in the closing stages and even a late goal from Donegal substitute Brian McLoughlin failed to dampen the enthusiasm of the men from Breffni. Cavan goalkeeper Paul O'Dowd played superbly and brought off a number of fine saves throughout the game, including two close-range attempts from James Ruane late in the game. Defenders Bernard Morris and Gerry Sheridan, along with midfielders Stephen King and Dermot McCabe and forwards Larry and Peter Reilly, also made significant contributions in what was a solid team performance by Cavan.

Martin McHugh joined me in the RTE Commentary box after the game and expressed himself well satisfied with Cavan's performance, particularly in the second-half. McHugh told me that he planned to have a few drinks with the Donegal players that night and let the Cavan players and supporters enjoy the celebrations.

Clearly a man who has not forgotten his roots and the place where he honed his football skills from a very early age. He may be manager of Cavan, but his heart is still very much in the homes of Donegal.

SCORERS - CAVAN: Ronan Carolan 1-7; Peter Reilly 1-2; Larry Reilly 0-4; Raymond Cunningham 0-1; Stephen King 0-1; Damien O'Reilly 0-1
DONEGAL: Manus Boyle 0-4; Tony Boyle 1-1; Brian McLoughlin 1-0; Brian Roper 0-2; Declan Bonner 0-2; Noel Hegarty 0-1

CAVAN

Paul O'Dowd

Ciaran Brady | Damien O'Reilly | Terry Farrelly

Gerry Sheridan | Bernard Morris | Patrick Sheils

Stephen King | Dermot McCabe

Raymond Cunningham | Ronan Carolan | Fintan Cahill

Peter Reilly | Larry Reilly | Mickey Graham

SUBSTITUTES: Philip Kermath for Damien O'Reilly; Damien O'Reilly for Mickey Graham; Anthony Forde for Peter Reilly

DONEGAL

Paul Callaghan

Peter McGinley | John Joe Doherty | Sean McEwen

Mark Crossan | Noel Hegarty | Martin Shovlin

Brian Murray | James Ruane

Jim McGuinness | Adrian Sweeney | John Ban Gallagher

Declan Bonner | Tony Boyle | Manus Boyle

SUBSTITUTES: Brian Roper for Adrian Sweeney; Brian McLoughlin for Declan Bonner; Damien Diver for Jim McGuinness

CAVAN
BACK ROW L TO R: Peter Reilly, Dermot McCabe, Terry Farrelly, Paul O'Dowd, Damien O'Reilly, Ronan Carolan, Patrick Sheils, Bernard Morris;
FRONT ROW L TO R: Larry Reilly, Raymond Cunningham, Mickey Graham, Stephen King, Gerry Sheridan, Fintan Cahill, Ciaran Brady.

DONEGAL
BACK ROW L TO R: Declan Bonner, Brian Murray, Paul Callaghan, James Ruane, Jim McGuinness, Tony Boyle, John Ban Gallagher;
FRONT ROW L TO R: Mark Crossan, Manus Boyle, Noel Hegarty, John Joe Doherty, Peter McGinley, Martin Shovlin,
Sean McEwen, Adrian Sweeney.

SUNDAY, JUNE 29, 1997

ULSTER SENIOR FOOTBALL CHAMPIONSHIP SEMI-FINAL

DERRY versus TYRONE

ST. TIGHEARNACH'S PARK, CLONES

REFEREE: PAT McENANEY (MONAGHAN)

RESULT: DERRY 2-15 TYRONE 2-3

THE WHEELS CAME OFF the Tyrone bandwagon in dramatic fashion as brilliant Derry scored an emphatic twelve points victory over their keenest rivals. Champions Tyrone, seeking their third provincial title in a row, played well-below-par and consequently suffered a very embarrassing defeat. Derry were the masters in most every sector of the field and exploited every Tyrone weakness to the full. It was a strangely lethargic display by Tyrone and the team looked weary from two energy-sapping, but failed adventures on the national stage in '95 and '96. Every team needs tangible reward to spur them on and Tyrone surely deserved more than two Ulster Championship titles for their supreme efforts. A first All-Ireland senior title would have changed everything!

Having lost to Tyrone at the semi-final stages of both the '95 and '96 Ulster Championships, Derry's more experienced players were only too well aware of the consequences of yet another defeat.

It looked gloomy for the men from the Oak Leaf county early on when Noel Donnelly, one of the all-too-few Tyrone players to enhance his reputation, latched on to a pass from Peter Canavan and crashed the ball to the net past Damien McCusker for a stunning goal. But then everything changed. Changed utterly!

Tyrone only scored once more before half-time, an Adrian Cush free on 35 minutes, by which time Derry had tacked on no-less-than eight points. Tyrone won plenty of good possession in the early exchanges, but failed miserably to utilise it. Derry started nervously, but it soon became apparent that speedy wing-back Gary Coleman was going to have a major influence on the game. Coleman's two points from play helped to get the well-oiled Derry machine motoring at a stage when both sides were struggling to gain supremacy.

Once Anthony Tohill began to dominate midfield, the whole pattern of the game changed entirely. Tohill edged Derry ahead for the first time after 24 minutes and thereafter the result was never in doubt. The Derry forwards had a field day! Joe Brolly, Joe Cassidy and Seamus Downey set about their task with relish against a Tyrone backline, which, apart from Noel Donnelly, was leaden-footed and ill at ease. Derry were on fire whereas Tyrone looked burnt-out!

Cassidy extended Derry's lead with two splendidly taken points from play before 'smiling Joe', the cheekiest forward in the game, took a pass from Dermot Dougan and scored his third goal in three games. And off he went again on his kissing crusade! And well he might!

Derry were now nine points clear and in the mood for exacting revenge for the previous two years. Tyrone rallied briefly when Mattie McGleenan struck a powerful shot to the net past the reach of McCusker for only the champions' third score in over forty-minutes, and just their second from play.

Tohill continued to prove his pedigree as one of the finest midfielders in the land while Brolly, Cassidy and Seamus Downey ran the Tyrone defence ragged. Downey scored Derry's second goal ten minutes from time to completely demoralise the opposition.

McGleenan's goal apart, Peter Canavan accounted for Tyrone's meagre total of two points in the second-half as the defending champions surrendered their crown in untypically tame fashion. Naturally enough, Derry were all smiles after delivering their most impressive victory since their 1993 All-Ireland Final success against Cork.

SCORERS - DERRY: Joe Brolly 1-4; Joe Cassidy 0-4; Seamus Downey 1-0; Gary Coleman 0-2; Anthony Tohill 0-2; Seán Martin Lockhart 0-1; Dermot Heaney 0-1; Fergal McCusker 0-1
TYRONE: Noel Donnelly 1-0; Mattie McGleenan 1-0; Peter Canavan 0-2; Adrian Cush 0-1

DERRY

Damien McCusker

Kieran McKeever | David O'Neill | Johnny McBride

Seán Martin Lockhart | Henry Downey | Gary Coleman

Anthony Tohill | Dermot Heaney

Gary McGill | Dermot Dougan | Fergal McCusker

Joe Brolly | Seamus Downey | Joe Cassidy

SUBSTITUTES: Brian McCormick for Gary McGill; Karl Diamond for Seán Martin Lockhart

TYRONE

Finbar McConnell

Fay Devlin | Chris Lawn | Paul Devlin

Noel Donnelly | Fergal Logan | Ronan McGarrity

Enda Kilpatrick | Seamus McCallan

Adrian Cush | Pascal Canavan | Brian Dooher

Mattie McGleenan | Stephen Lawn | Peter Canavan

SUBSTITUTES: Gerard Cavlan for Brian Dooher; Sean McLoughlin for Paul Devlin; Ciaran McBride for Mattie McGleenan

DERRY
BACK ROW L TO R: Gary McGill, Anthony Tohill, Damien McCusker, Dermot Heaney, David O'Neill, Dermot Dougan, Joe Brolly;
FRONT ROW L TO R: Seamus Downey, Fergal McCusker, Seán Martin Lockhart, Henry Downey, Kieran McKeever, Gary Coleman, Johnny McBride, Joe Cassidy.

TYRONE
BACK ROW L TO R: Paul Devlin, Jody Gormley, Adrian Cush, Gerard Cavlan, Seamus McCallan, Finbar McConnell, Enda Kilpatrick, Brian Dooher, Fergal Logan, Paul Donnelly, Joe Cassidy, Ciaran McBride;
FRONT ROW L TO R: Mattie McGleenan, Ronan McGarrity, Stephen Lawn, Peter Canavan, Noel Donnelly, Chris Lawn, Pascal Canavan, Fay Devlin.
SITTING L TO R: Paul O'Neill, Ciaran Loughran, Benny Owens.

SUNDAY, JULY 20, 1997

ULSTER SENIOR FOOTBALL CHAMPIONSHIP FINAL

CAVAN versus DERRY

ST. TIGHEARNACH'S PARK, CLONES

REFEREE: PAT McENANEY (MONAGHAN)

RESULT: CAVAN 1-14 DERRY 0-16

CAVAN EMERGED FROM a twenty-eight-year wilderness around the football fields of Ulster to claim their 39th provincial Championship with a one point win over favourites, Derry, in a truly riveting game at Clones. There were highly emotional and joyous scenes after the game as thousands upon thousands of blue-and-white clad Cavan supporters literally danced with delight on the Clones pitch. A never-to-be-forgotten occasion! Nearly three decades of pent-up emotion was released and the noise reached a crescendo when Cavan captain, Stephen King, raised the Anglo Celt Cup to the heavens. The weight of a lifetime was lifted off the shoulders of every true blue Cavan follower who had come to despair of such a happy day ever arriving again. Young and old alike cheered and roared with wild abandon. And it took a proud Donegal man, Martin McHugh, to unlock the door and come up with a successful formula to end Cavan's misery around the football fields of Ulster.

McHugh, the former Donegal All-Ireland medal winner, instilled great self-belief in his players and that was particularly evident in the closing stages as Derry fought tooth-and-nail to rescue the game after substitute Jason Reilly scored the only goal of the game.

Football was the real winner at Clones as both sides ran themselves to a standstill in search of glory. Cavan forwards constantly created openings in a none-too-assured Derry defence which struggled to contain chief tormentors Larry and Peter Reilly. At the other end of the field, All-Star Joe Brolly was finding the going tough against Gerry Sheridan, who had the onerous task of keeping tabs on the Dungiven marksman. Cavan captain Stephen King suffered a hamstring injury early in the game which greatly restricted his movement, but his midfield partner, Dermot McCabe, rose to the challenge with a superb display. King was forced to move into the full-forward line in a direct swap with Damien O'Reilly before being replaced in the second-half by Philip Smith. The Cavan backs at all times defended stoutly and never allowed the Derry forwards the space to showcase their undoubted class. It was an absorbing encounter which ebbed and flowed until the sound of Pat McEnaney's whistle called a halt to proceedings and sent Cavan supporters into ecstasy.

The sides were level on no-less-than eight occasions in the first half alone during which Ronan Carolan pointed three frees and made a considerable all-round contribution for Cavan. Carolan, who failed to get into the starting fifteen in the early rounds of the Championship, landed three more points in the second-half to underline his immense worth to Cavan.

The Cavan forwards missed a number of scoring chances in the first-half which, if converted, could have settled the issue much earlier.

Fintan Cahill sent over the first point of the second-half and two more from Carolan left Cavan ahead by three points by the 40th minute. But, typically, Derry stormed back with points from Gary Mc Gill, Gary Coleman and Brolly to level the game for the ninth time. Peter Reilly restored Cavan's lead with a point from a free and soon afterwards Carolan landed his sixth point of the game. Then came a Derry spell of dominance that could have destroyed lesser teams. Defender Johnny McBride and Anthony Tohill fired over a point each and then Kieran McKeever finished a superb sweeping move to fist over the lead point. Cavan applied themselves once more and substitute Jason Reilly scored the decisive goal to spark off massive celebrations.

Cavan were forced to defend heroically in the closing minutes and goalkeeper Paul O'Dowd had to produce a stunning save to deprive Derry a goal. Joe Brolly scored a late point for Derry to reduce the margin to a single point in what was an enthralling game. Soon after, the final whistle sounded and jubilant Cavan supporters swarmed on to St. Tighearnach's Park. Stephen King collected the Anglo Celt Cup and Croke Park braced itself for Cavan's return after a gap of twenty-eight years. Dreams do after all come true!

SCORERS - CAVAN: Ronan Carolan 0-6; Peter Reilly 0-3; Jason Reilly 1-0; Larry Reilly 0-2; Fintan Cahill 0-1; Dermot McCabe 0-1; Raymond Cunningham 0-1
DERRY: Anthony Tohill 0-4; Joe Brolly 0-3; Gary Coleman 0-2; Gary McGill 0-2; Fergal McCusker 0-1; Dermot Dougan 0-1, Kieran McKeever 0 1; Johnny McBride 0-1; Joe Cassidy 0-1

CAVAN

Paul O'Dowd

Philip Kermath — Ciaran Brady — Gerry Sheridan
Terry Farrelly — Bernard Morris — Patrick Sheils
Stephen King — Dermot McCabe
Peter Reilly — Ronan Carolan — Raymond Cunningham
Larry Reilly — Fintan Cahill — Damien O'Reilly

SUBSTITUTES: Jason Reilly for Fintan Cahill;
Philip Smith for Stephen King; Mickey Graham for Larry Reilly

DERRY

Damien McCusker

Kieran McKeever — David O'Neill — Johnny McBride
Seán Martin Lockhart — Henry Downey — Gary Coleman
Anthony Tohill — Dermot Heaney
Gary Magill — Dermot Dougan — Fergal McCusker
Joe Brolly — Seamus Downey — Joe Cassidy

SUBSTITUTES: Gary Doyle for Gary Magill; Karl Diamond for Dermot Dougan

CAVAN

BACK ROW L TO R: Peter Reilly, Dermot McCabe, Terry Farrelly, Ronan Carolan, Paul O'Dowd, Patrick Sheils, Damien O'Reilly, Bernard Morris;
FRONT ROW L TO R: Ciaran Brady, Gerry Sheridan, Larry Reilly, Stephen King, Fintan Cahill, Philip Kermath, Raymond Cunningham.

DERRY

BACK ROW L TO R: Seamus Downey, Gary McGill, Anthony Tohill, Damien McCusker, Dermot Heaney, Dermot Dougan, Joe Brolly;
BACK ROW L TO R: Fergal McCusker, Seán Martin Lockhart, Henry Downey, Kieran McKeever, Gary Coleman, Johnny McBride, David O'Neill, Joe Cassidy.

SUNDAY, AUGUST 24, 1997

ALL-IRELAND SENIOR FOOTBALL CHAMPIONSHIP SEMI-FINAL

KERRY versus CAVAN

CROKE PARK

REFEREE: PAT CASSERLY (WESTMEATH)

RESULT: KERRY 1-17 CAVAN 1-10

KERRY HAD JUST QUALIFIED for their first All-Ireland final since 1986 and Páidí Ó Sé was grinning from ear to ear. He chased here and there around Croke Park, followed by hordes of delighted Kerry supporters, in search of the players that had ended the eleven-year famine. The Kerry manager, beads of perspiration on his face, was in seventh heaven and waxing lyrical: "If you sail to the Blaskets once, you're bound to learn a lot and the trip will be easier the second time round. We learned a valuable lesson against Mayo last year and we put it to good use today."

Kerry came in for some severe criticism after their six points defeat by Mayo in last year's All-Ireland semi-final and this made the players even more determined to deliver a match-winning performance. Kerry players never like to lose and their supporters are never slow to remind them of the unrivalled success of their predecessors. Much is demanded of those who wear the green and gold Kerry jersey.

This present Kerry team have learned from their past mistakes and are not that far off the finished article. The Kingdom can boast potential match-winners in All-Star Maurice Fitzgerald, unquestionably the most naturally gifted player in Gaelic Football, Seamus Moynihan, Dara Ó Sé and Pa Laide and, add to that, the genius of super-sub, Michael Francis Russell. Here is a player of exceptional talent. His splendidly taken goal late in the game ended any hopes of a Cavan revival. Billy O'Shea made a huge impact when introduced in place of the injured Denis O'Dwyer, who suffered concussion after a very heavy fall. O'Shea's pace helped open up the Cavan defence and the Laune Rangers player also scored two points from play as well as setting up scores for his colleagues.

The lightning-fast Cavan forwards exposed weaknesses in a creaking Kerry defence which was caught for pace in the early stages of the game. Stephen King had a fine first-half for Cavan, winning a lot of possession, while his midfield partner, Dermot McCabe landed two points. William Kirby and Dara Ó Sé improved significantly as the game wore on and both played a key role in Kerry's victory.

Croke Park was turned into a sea of blue and white when Stephen King led Cavan on to the field. Few teams, if any, have ever received such a warm and colourful welcome. The noise was simply deafening. 28 years is a mighty long time! Although Ronan Carolan edged Cavan in front with an early pointed free, Kerry had established a 0-3 to 0-1 lead after just six minutes with a point each from Dara Ó Sé, Denis O'Dwyer and Pa Laide. The Cavan forwards were first to the ball in many instances and with the Kerry defence under constant pressure and tending to foul, the Ulster Champions had moved ahead by the 13th minute through points from Carolan and Larry and Peter Reilly. Kerry goal-keeper, Declan O'Keeffe, outstanding all through the game, brought off a superb save to deprive Peter Reilly a certain goal. That save was a turning point.

Maurice Fitzgerald was now roaming out from his corner-forward position and gaining good possession. The brilliant All-Star scored three points without reply and shortly afterwards, Eamonn Breen had a goal disallowed after running on to a quick free from Brian Clarke. The referee called play back and awarded a free which Fitzgerald converted. Fintan Cahill scored a magnificent goal for Cavan deep into injury-time in the first half to put the Ulster Champions 1-7 to 0-9 ahead at half-time.

The goal failed to deflate the Kerrymen and they came storming out of the blocks at the start of the second-half with a point from replacement captain, Liam Hassett, and two more from Maurice Fitzgerald. Morgan O'Shea replaced Seán Burke at half-time and his introduction helped strenghten the Kerry full-back line. Cavan persisted with their short passing game and Kerry substitute, Billy O'Shea, and Seamus Moynihan won a lot of breaking ball to thwart and frustrate the oppostion.

Brave Cavan, to their credit, battled back to draw level by the 47th minute with points from Cahill and Damien O'Reilly but it was an uphill struggle from there to the finish for the men of Breffni. Cavan scored just one point for the remainder of the game and their hopes of advancing to the final were dashed when substitute Jason Reilly was denied a penalty after being dragged to the ground. Shortly afterwards, Michael Francis Russell hit home a wonder goal, Kerry's first score for nearly quarter of an hour; Fitzgerald tacked on a point and then set up young Russell, who made it a memorable day for himself and all of Kerry with the final point of the game. Cavan hardly deserved to lose by seven points, but there was no doubting Kerry's second-half superiority when they outscored the Ulster Champions by 1-8 to 0-3 points. Ten players scored for Kerry to underline the value of a team performance. Job well done for the Kingdom. But some improvement required before a 31st All-Ireland title can be secured!

SCORERS - KERRY: Maurice Fitzgerald 0-7; Michael Francis Russell 1-1; Billy O'Shea 0-2; Dara Ó Sé 0-1; Denis O'Dwyer 0-1; Brian Clarke 0-1; Pa Laide 0-1; Liam Hassett 0-1; Eamonn Breen 0-1; Dara Ó Cinnéide 0-1
CAVAN: Ronan Carolan 0-4; Fintan Cahill 1-1; Dermot McCabe 0-2; Damien O'Reilly 0-1; Larry Reilly 0-1; Peter Reilly 0-1

KERRY

Declan O'Keeffe

Seán Burke — Barry O'Shea — Stephen Stack

Eamonn Breen — Liam O'Flaherty — Seamus Moynihan

Dara Ó Sé — William Kirby

Pa Laide — Liam Hassett — Denis O'Dwyer

Dara Ó Cinnéide — Brian Clarke — Maurice Fitzgerald

SUBSTITUTES: Billy O'Shea for Denis O'Dwyer;
Morgan O'Shea for Seán Burke; Michael Francis Russell for Brian Clarke

CAVAN

	Paul O'Dowd	
Terry Farrelly	Ciaran Brady	Philip Kermath
Patrick Sheils	Bernard Morris	Gerry Sheridan
Stephen King		Dermot McCabe
Peter Reilly	Ronan Carolan	Raymond Cunningham
Larry Reilly	Fintan Cahill	Damien O'Reilly

SUBSTITUTES: Jason Reilly for Patrick Sheils;
Philip Smith for Ronan Carolan; Mickey Graham for Larry Reilly

KERRY
BACK ROW L TO R: Dara Ó Sé, Barry O'Shea, Seán Burke, Liam O'Flaherty, Maurice Fitzgerald, Brian Clarke, William Kirby, Stephen Stack;
FRONT ROW L TO R: Pa Laide, Eamonn Breen, Seamus Moynihan, Liam Hassett, Declan O'Keeffe, Denis O'Dwyer, Dara Ó Cinnéide.

CAVAN
BACK ROW L TO R: Peter Reilly, Dermot McCabe, Terry Farrelly, Ronan Carolan, Paul O'Dowd, Patrick Sheils, Damien O'Reilly, Larry Reilly, Bernard Morris;
FRONT ROW L TO R: Gerry Sheridan, Raymond Cunningham, Stephen King, Fintan Cahill, Philip Kermath, Ciaran Brady.

SUNDAY, AUGUST 31, 1997

ALL-IRELAND SENIOR FOOTBALL SEMI-FINAL

MAYO versus OFFALY

CROKE PARK

REFEREE: PADDY RUSSELL (TIPPERARY)

RESULT: MAYO 0-13 OFFALY 0-7

THERE WERE POSITIVE ASPECTS about Mayo's performance which were absent in the course of their narrow one-point win over Sligo in the Connacht Final, but equally there were other factors to cause concern for manager John Maughan on a day when his team made heavy work of disposing of the challenge of an out-of-sorts Offaly side.

Their below-par display in the provincial decider raised serious questions about Mayo's all-round ability, but this improved showing against Offaly served to highlight their many strengths as much as to expose their weaknesses.

Physically stronger, Mayo were the dominant team throughout the entire game, but yet were only six points ahead at the finish despite an abundance of possession. Seventeen wides bear testimony to Mayo's squandermania and that particular facet of their play will have to be significantly improved if Kerry are to be beaten in the final. A big increase in the forward scoring rate is imperative if Mayo are to bridge a 46-year gap and win their first All-Ireland title since 1951.

Offaly failed to reproduce their stunning Leinster Final form due in large part to the superb display of the Mayo defence and Pat Fallon's superiority at midfield. Fallon ruled the roost with a superlative display of high-fielding which, allied to his excellent positional play and first-rate distribution, gave Mayo an advantage they never conceded.

James Nallen and Fergal Costello were oustanding in the Mayo half-back line while captain Noel Connelly was also very effective. With Mayo in control at midfield and in the half-back area, the much vaunted Offaly full-forward line rarely got a good supply of ball to prove their capabilities. Roy Malone, Vinny Claffey and Peter Brady scored 3-8 between them against Meath in the Leinster Final, yet the highly-rated trio could only muster a single point against Mayo. The potency of their full-forward line was diminished and Offaly suffered as a consequence. Great credit must be given also to the Mayo full-back division for their all-round display in curbing Offaly's most lethal scoring line. But there were other factors which accounted for Offaly's mediocre display. The wet and windy conditions certainly militated against the lighter Offaly players and their inexperience was also evident from an early stage. Whenever and wherever an Offaly player gained possession, he was immediately put under pressure and harassed into giving the ball away too quickly.

With wind advantage, Mayo completely dominated the first-half and were 0-7 to 0-2 ahead at the interval. The margin would have been considerably greater but for some waywardness in front of goal by the Mayo forwards. Liam McHale kicked the opening point for Mayo and the tactic of playing the All-Star midfielder at full-forward worked out well in the early stages as he had the measure of Larry Carroll. However, full-back Carroll continued to battle for every ball and emerged as one of Offaly's better players in the second-half. By the 16th minute, Mayo had moved four points to no score ahead through a point each from Kieran McDonald, David Nestor and Pat Fallon. Maurice Sheridan, showing no ill effects from a hamstring injury, rowed in with a good point from a free. The Balla club man was also very effective in general play. By the time impressive wing-back Fergal Costello landed his first point after 23 minutes, Mayo had moved six points clear with Offaly still to score.

Offaly came close to scoring a goal after eighteen minutes when Peter Brady's fisted effort almost caught out Mayo goalkeeper, Peter Burke, who somehow got the ball away to safety.

Colm Quinn finally got Offaly off the mark with a point from play after 24 minutes and David Reynolds followed up with a point from a free eight minutes later to reduce the margin to four points. Sheridan converted his second free in injury-time to leave Mayo five points ahead at the interval, but questions remained whether the margin would be sufficent for the Connacht Champions, who had to face the breeze in the second-half.

Offaly full-forward, Roy Malone, so devastating against Meath, missed a gilt-edged chance of a goal within a minute of the re-start. Malone got inside the Mayo defence, but he miskicked the ball when a goal seemed the certain outcome. Peter Brady and Maurice Sheridan swapped points before David Reynolds sent over his second free to reduce the deficit to four points. But Offaly were never able to make a telling impact even as Mayo continued to squander chances. As the game wore on, it became more and more evident that only a goal would salvage Offaly's Championship ambitions. Kieran McDonald scored two excellent points from play to push Mayo six points clear with only twelve minutes remaining. Substitute Kevin O'Neill made a significant contributon in bolstering the Mayo attack when introduced in place of James Horan early in the second-half. Offaly twice reduced the margin to four points in the closing ten minutes, but each time Mayo hit back with telling scores of their own to demoralise the Leinster Champions.

David Nestor and Maurice Sheridan rounded off the scoring with a point each to send Mayo through to their second successive All-Ireland Final for the first time 1950 and '51.

SCORERS - MAYO: Maurice Sheridan 0-4; Kieran McDonald 0-3; David Nestor 0-2; Liam McHale 0-1; Fergal Costello 0-1; Pat Fallon 0-1; Kevin O'Neill 0-1
OFFALY: David Reynolds 0-4; Peter Brady 0-1; Colm Quinn 0-1; James Grennan 0-1

MAYO

Peter Burke

Kenneth Mortimer — Pat Holmes — Dermot Flanagan

Fergal Costello — James Nallen — Noel Connelly

Pat Fallon — David Heaney

David Nestor — Colm McManamon — James Horan

Kieran McDonald — Liam McHale — Maurice Sheridan

SUBSTITUTES: Kevin O'Neill for James Horan;
P.J. Loftus for Maurice Sheridan

OFFALY

Padraig Kelly

Cathal Daly | Larry Carroll | Barry Malone

John Kenny | Finbar Cullen | Tom Coffey

Ronan Mooney | Seán Grennan

Colm Quinn | Ciaran McManus | David Reynolds

Vinny Claffey | Roy Malone | Peter Brady

SUBSTITUTES: James Grennan for Ciaran McManus; Mark Daly for Colm Quinn; Vincent Mooney for Roy Malone

MAYO
BACK ROW L TO R: Liam McHale, Pat Holmes, Kieran McDonald, Pat Fallon, Peter Burke, Maurice Sheridan, James Nallen, James Horan;
FRONT ROW L TO R: David Nestor, Fergal Costello, Kenneth Mortimer, Noel Connelly, Dermot Flanagan, Colm McManamon, David Heaney.

OFFALY
BACK ROW L TO R: Larry Carroll, John Kenny, Peter Brady, Seán Grennan, Colm Quinn, Roy Malone, Ciaran McManus;
FRONT ROW L TO R: Cathal Daly, David Reynolds, Tom Coffey, Barry Malone, Finbar Cullen, Ronan Mooney, Padraig Kelly, Vinny Claffey.

SUNDAY, SEPTEMBER 14, 1997

ALL-IRELAND SENIOR HURLING FINAL

CLARE versus TIPPERARY

CROKE PARK

REFEREE: DICKIE MURPHY (WEXFORD)

RESULT: CLARE 0-20 TIPPERARY 2-13

THIS WAS AN All-Ireland Final to remember - an exhilarating game, brimful of passion, skill, bravery commitment and nerve-jangling tension that had the 65,575 crowd in Croke Park on the edge of their seats throughout. Clare manager Ger Loughnane described it as "the greatest game of hurling I have ever seen. An epic, epic All-Ireland Final."

Sure enough, this was yet another momentous occasion for the mighty hurling men from the Banner county. Saffron and blue was the colour as thousands upon thousands of deliriously happy Clare supporters cheered, sang, danced and beat bodhrans to their hearts content as Anthony Daly lifted the Liam McCarthy Cup on the steps of the Hogan Stand for the second-time. It was like 1995 all over again! Even Tony Considine sang a verse of the Banner anthem, 'My Lovely Rose Of Clare'.

But it could all have been so different. Put simply, what a world of difference a save makes! Tipperary made an immense contribution to this epic encounter and only a truly magnificent save by brilliant Clare goalkeeper Davy Fitzgerald denied Len Gaynor's courageous team victory in this unique All-Munster, All-Ireland Hurling Final.

John Leahy, who had the misfortune to mis-hit a ball from close-range in the closing stages of the Munster Final which Clare won by three points, had a gilt-edged chance to seal a sensational victory in those last tension-filled seconds. Leahy gathered a long ball from Brian O'Meara and with nothing less than a goal on his mind, drove the ball low and hard to the left corner. Everyone in Croke Park and millions watching on television held their breath and the relief on the faces of Clare players and supporters alike was palpable when Fitzgerald, a small man with a big heart, somehow got his hurley to the ball for a spectacular save. Moments later, Conor Gleeson had the chance of an equalising point, but his long-range effort sailed wide and Clare were hurling kingpins once again.

The game was as dramatic as it was tense. Clare won this gripping encounter without scoring a goal, but some of their point scoring was nothing short of breathtaking. Coincidentally, the last team to win a senior All-Ireland Hurling Final without scoring a goal was Tipperary, who defeated Dublin by a single point, 0-16 to 1-12, back in 1961.

Tipperary scored two goals, their second from full-forward Eugene O'Neill edging the Premier county one point ahead with less than five minutes remaining. Man of the Match Ollie Baker levelled the game with a splendid point from play and Jamesie O'Connor restored Clare's lead with what proved to be the last score of the game. It was fitting that O'Connor should deliver the winning point as he was one of Clare's outstanding players throughout Championship '97. With time running out, Tippeary continued to press forward in search of scores and Leahy would have emerged the hero of heroes but for Fitzgerald's ultra-sharp reflexes. The Sixmilebridge goalkeeper told me afterwards: "I knew the minute he took the ball in his hand that he was going for a goal, but I just concentrated on keeping my eye on the ball and thankfully it worked out well."

Some Tipperary supporters felt Leahy should have taken his point, but Len Gaynor, one of the real gentlemen of sport, told me in the dressingroom after the game that his star forward made the correct decision and those sentiments were echoed by his team-mates.

The last-minute drama involving Leahy and Fitzgerald will forever be etched in the memory of those who watched it unfold. Praise galore for Fitzgerald, nothing but sympathy for Leahy. The reverse would have been the case had the net danced. The unconfined joy and total agony of sport encapsulated in a mere few seconds.

Just one point separated the sides at the finish which served to highlight an incident in the first-half when Tipperary centre-half-forward, Declan Ryan, appeared to score a point from play. One umpire raised his hand as if to indicate a point, while the other signalled wide. Referee Dickie Murphy consulted with the umpire and no flag was raised.

There were no complaints to be heard afterwards from the Tipperary players and management team. Typically, they were magnaminous in defeat and even in their gloom gave full credit to Clare for their magnificent achievement. Neither was there any triumphalism from Clare, just a deep satisfaction of a job well done. All round, hurling was the real winner.

This was a game Clare wanted to win badly and with victories over Cork, Tipperary (twice) and Kilkenny to their credit in Championship '97, no one can deny the Banner men their right to be hailed the best hurling team in the land.

Although Len Gaynor and Ger Loughnane had been confined to the dug-outs because of previous incursions on the field, it was decided that benches would be placed near the sideline for the two managers. But the green seats were soon vacated by both men when the tension heightened and Ger Loughnane had his name taken late in the second-half for a pitch infringement.

There was drama even before the throw-in when it emerged that Niall Gilligan would play at corner-forward instead of Fergal Hegarty. It was the best-kept secret of the year, perhaps the decade! Sixteen Clare players lined up for the customary pre-match photograph, but it was Gilligan who marched behind the Artane Boys Band.

Although Seán McMahon landed an early free for Clare, it soon became evident that Tipperary were winning many of the individual battles around the field. By the eighth minute, Tipperary, favoured by a stiff breeze, had three points on the scoreboard, one each from Michael Cleary, Tommy Dunne and Brian O'Meara, whose superb individual score was symptomatic of the way the game was developing. Clare shot three wides in the opening ten minutes, but Ollie Baker gave us an inkling of things to come with a well-taken point from play.

The Tipperary defence, spearheaded by Paul Shelly and Conal Bonnar, had the measure of the Clare forwards, while in attack, John Leahy and Declan Ryan were in sparkling form. Eugene O'Neill was proving more than a handful for Brian Lohan while Tommy Dunne was playing his part at midfield as Tipperary slowly but surely took a grip on the game.

Tipperary had increased their lead to six points, 0-9 to 0-3, after 27 minutes play when Fergal Hegarty was introduced in place of Fergus Tuohy. Niall Gilligan was switched to left-corner-forward and he prospered in his new role. Jamesie O'Connor scored his first point of the day and rejuvenated Gilligan brought Clare right back into contention with two superb points from play.

The in-form Leahy replied with a point to leave Tipperary 0-10 to 0-6 ahead at the interval, but facing a strong breeze in the second-half. Those three late, first-half points were vitally important for Clare as they served to reverse the trend of the game and prove a real confidence booster.

Clare gained a psychological advantage immediately after the re-start when Liam Doyle raced up field and landed a splendid point after barely ten seconds. Conor Clancy delivered his first point of the game and Ger 'Sparrow' O'Loughlin did likewise to continue Clare's revival. Lightning-fast Jamesie O'Connor was now in full flight, while midfielder Ollie Baker was hurling his heart out. This was the Ollie of old. Perhaps even a shade better.

The impressive Tommy Dunne hit over a free for Tipperary, but a point each from O'Connor and midfielder Colin Lynch brought the sides level for only the second time after 42 minutes. The pendulum had swung in favour of the Clare men. Jamesie O'Connor continued to find the target; substitute David Forde landed two points while Gilligan hit over his second point. That scoring flurry left Clare 0-17 to 0-12 ahead and well in control with fourteen minutes remaining.

But Tipp were far from finished. Leahy converted a free and substitute Liam Cahill kicked the sliotar to the net. Suddenly just one point separated the sides. O'Connor edged Clare two points clear before Tommy Dunne's '65 came off the crossbar and Eugene O'Neill crashed the rebound to the net. Almost immediately, Ollie Baker sent over the equalising point and soon afterwards Colin Lynch delivered a pass to O'Connor who whipped over what proved to be the match- winning point. Leahy had a glorious chance to snatch victory for Tipperary, but Fitzgerald made that never-to-be-forgotten save. Conor Gleeson's long-range effort went wide and Clare were 1997 All-Ireland Hurling Champions!

Tens of thousands of fanatical supporters greeted Ger Loughanane and his all-conquering heroes on their arrival in Clare on Monday night with the Liam McCarthy Cup. It was a unique occasion as Clare minors were also feted after completing an historic double.

Quite a hectic week for All-Ireland winning captain, Anthony Daly, as he married Eilis Murphy from the village of Connolly on the Saturday following Clare's magnificent victory. The end of a week and the end of a Championship that Captain Fantastic will never, ever forget!

SCORERS - CLARE: Jamesie O'Connor 0-7; Niall Gilligan 0-3; David Forde 0-2; Ollie Baker 0-2; Colin Lynch 0-2; Seán McMahon 0-1; Liam Doyle 0-1;Ger O'Loughlin 0-1; Conor Clancy 0-1
TIPPERARY: Thomas Dunne 0-5; Eugene O'Neill 1-1; John Leahy 0-4; Liam Cahill 1-0; Michael Cleary 0-1; Brian O'Meara 0-1; Conor Gleeson 0-1

CLARE

Davy Fitzgerald

Michael O'Halloran	Brian Lohan	Frank Lohan
Liam Doyle	Sean McMahon	Anthony Daly
Ollie Baker		Colin Lynch
Jamesie O'Connor	Conor Clancy	P.J. O'Connell
Niall Gilligan	Ger O'Loughlin	Fergus Tuohy

SUBSTITUTES: Fergal Hegarty for Fergus Tuohy; David Forde for P.J. O'Connell; Barry Murphy for Fergal Hegarty

TIPPERARY

Brendan Cummins

Paul Shelly	Noel Sheehy	Michael Ryan
Liam Sheedy	Colm Bonnar	Conal Bonnar
Thomas Dunne		Conor Gleeson
Liam McGrath	Declan Ryan	John Leahy
Michael Cleary	Eugene O'Neill	Brian O'Meara

SUBSTITUTES: Aidan Ryan for Liam McGrath; Liam Cahill for Michael Cleary

CLARE
BACK ROW L TO R: Brian Lohan, Michael O'Halloran, Colin Lynch, Frank Lohan, Davy Fitzgerald, Conor Clancy, Fergal Hegarty, Ger O'Loughlin, Seán McMahon;
FRONT ROW L TO R: Liam Doyle, Ollie Baker, Anthony Daly, Jamesie O'Connor, P.J. O'Connell, Fergus Tuohy, Niall Gilligan.

TIPPERARY
BACK ROW L TO R: Thomas Dunne, Brian O'Meara, Noel Sheehy, Brendan Cummins, Michael Ryan, Liam Sheedy, Conal Bonnar;
FRONT ROW L TO R: Michael Cleary, Eugene O'Neill, John Leahy, Paul Shelly, Conor Gleeson, Liam McGrath, Declan Ryan, Colm Bonnar.

SUNDAY, MAY 18, 1997

MUNSTER SENIOR HURLING CHAMPIONSHIP QUARTER-FINAL

CLARE versus KERRY

CUSACK PARK, ENNIS

REFEREE: MICHAEL WADDING (WATERFORD)

RESULT: CLARE 3-24 KERRY 1-6

A TWENTY-FOUR POINTS victory tells its own story! Rampant Clare took control early on and completely overwhelmed a feeble Kerry team that was simply out its depth at this level. Things have got progressively worse for the hurlers of Kerry over the past two years. In 1995, Cork beat them by thirteen points and last year Tipperary had fourteen points to spare in their semi-final meeting at Tralee. To their credit, Kerry battled to the finish as one would expect from a team managed by John Meyler, who has worked extremely hard with the players at his disposal over the past five years. Just seven of the team that lined out against Tipperary last year were in action against Clare and the loss of key scoring forward, Brendan O'Sullivan, was another setback Meyler could have done without.

Conversely, Clare were dominant in most positions, but manager Ger Loughnane knows full well that the preliminaries are now over and the action will begin in earnest against Cork in the next round.

Kerry started brightly and more than held their own in the opening exchanges which saw the sides level 0-3 apiece after 11 minutes. But then, Clare scored five points without reply, including two from Jamesie O'Connor, to set the trend for the remainder of the game.

Wing-forward P.J. O'Connell scored two goals in a four-minute spell to push Clare twelve points clear and put the game out of the reach of Kerry with still some ten minutes remaining in the first-half.

Kerry rallied with a fine goal from Jerry O'Sullivan but Clare corner-forward Niall Gilligan completed the first-half scoring with a point from play to leave the Banner men 2-11 to 1-4 ahead at the interval.

Clare continued their dominance and outscored the opposition by 1-13 to 0-2 in an all-too one-sided second-half during which the 1995 All-Ireland Champions played some exhibition hurling. Conor Clancy scored Clare's third goal after 56 minutes and thereafter the Banner men struck over some text-book points from play to finish with a flourish.

SCORERS - CLARE: P.J. O'Connell 2-2; Jamesie O'Connor 0-6; Conor Clancy 1-2; Niall Gilligan 0-5; Seán McMahon 0-3; Ger O'Loughlin 0-2; Fergus Tuohy 0-2; Barry Murphy 0-1; David Forde 0-1
KERRY: Jerry O'Sullivan 1-0; M Slattery 0-2; T.J. Curran 0-1; Christy Walsh 0-1; B O'Mahony 0-1; Ian Maunsell 0-1

CLARE

Davy Fitzgerald

Michael O'Halloran — Brian Lohan — Brian Quinn

Liam Doyle — Sean McMahon — Anthony Daly

Colin Lynch — David Forde

Jamesie O'Connor — Conor Clancy — P.J. O'Connell

Niall Gilligan — Ger O'Loughlin — Barry Murphy

SUBSTITUTES: Fergus Tuohy for Jamesie O'Connor; Christy Chaplin for David Forde

KERRY

John Healy

Wille Joe Leen — Mike Casey — John Foley

Padraig Cronin — T.J. Curran — Ian Brick

Sean Fitzgerald — Tony Maunsell

Ian Maunsell — Christy Walsh — Brendan O'Mahony

Gerry O'Sullivan — Gary Frehill — Mike Slattery

SUBSTITUTES: Denis Harty for Brendan O'Mahony; Dan Harty for Willie Joe Leen; Tom O'Connell for Ian Brick

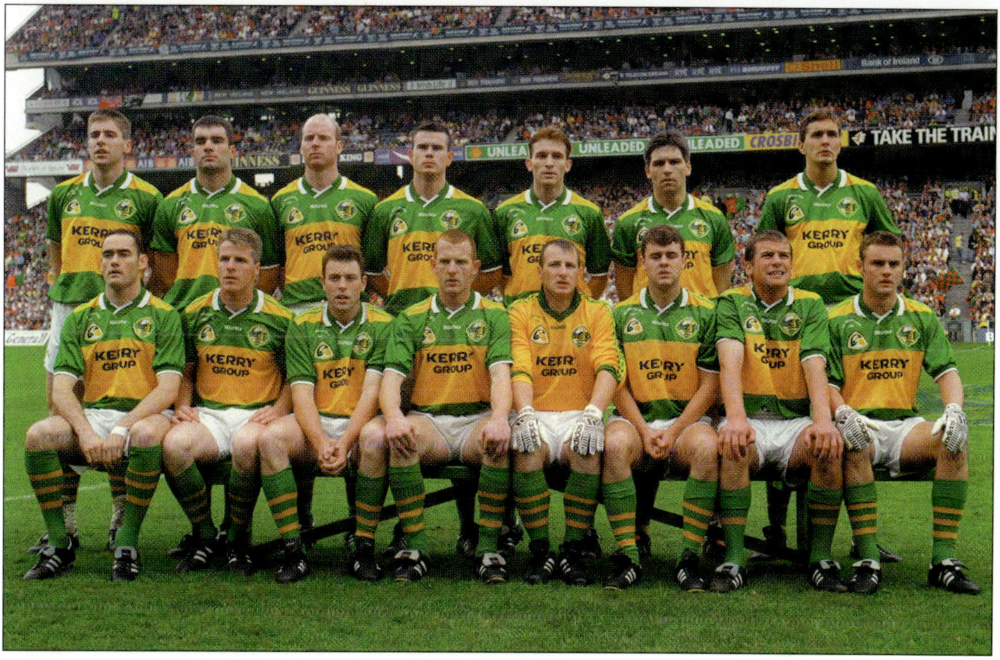

KERRY

BACK ROW L TO R: Dara Ó Sé, Barry O'Shea, Liam O'Flaherty, Killian Burns, Billy O'Shea, Stephen Stack, Maurice Fitzgerald;
FRONT ROW L TO R: Pa Laide, Eamonn Breen, Seamus Moynihan, Liam Hassett, Declan O'Keeffe, Denis O'Dwyer, Dara Ó Cinnéide, William Kirby.

CLARE

BACK ROW L TO R: Brian Lohan, Michael O'Halloran, Colin Lynch, Frank Lohan, Davy Fitzgerald, Conor Clancy, Fergal Hegarty, Ger O'Loughlin, Seán McMahon;
FRONT ROW L TO R: Liam Doyle, Ollie Baker, Anthony Daly, Jamesie O'Connor, P.J. O'Connell, Fergus Tuohy, Niall Gilligan.

A five tier Coaching qualification system is currently being implemented by the G.A.A. National Coaching and Games Development Committee. This involves the organisation of courses at Foundation Level (6 hours), Level 1 (20 hours), Level 2 (40 hours), Level 3 (200 hours), Level 4 (240 hours), Level 5 (360 hours). Coaches who successfully complete these courses will have access to an exclusive range of Coaching attire.

COACH EDUCATION PROGRAMME

The main distinguishing feature attaching to this attire, is the colour coding which has been introduced to denote the different levels: Yellow-Foundation; Red-Level 1; Green-Level 2; Maroon-Level 3; Purple-Level 4; Blue-Level 5. Apart from projecting positive and readily identifiable image, those who purchase this gear will also be making a contribution to advancing the aims and objectives of the G.A.A. Coaching Academy.

COACHING ACADEMY

For further information contact:

**Pat Daly, Coaching & Games Development Manager,
Cumann Lúthchleas Gael,
Croke Park, Jones' Road,
Dublin 3, Ireland.
Tel: 01-8363222. Fax: 01- 8366420.**

The look says it all. Maurice Fitzgerald on the move again despite the close attentions of Clare defender Padraig Gallagher.

It's mine all mine! Liam McHale is in control, but Offaly defenders Tom Coffey and Larry Carroll want a piece of the action.

Church & General
National Football
and Hurling Leagues
Cumann na mBunscol
Dedicated Supporter
Church & General
National Leagues

Happiness is ... Len Gaynor surrounded by jubilant Tipperary supporters.

Jamesie O'Connor and Liam Keoghan in perfect unison.

The Home Team.

You may miss being at the game, but you won't miss a single piece of the action with RTÉ's home team. (And if you do there's always action replay!)

RTÉ provides comprehensive GAA coverage and our team of expert commentators offers in-depth analysis on both Television and Radio.
It's an all round performance that's unbeatable.

RTÉ
RADIO TELEFIS EIREANN

No ordinary man! Kilkenny's hurling wizard, DJ Carey celebrates his second goal against Galway in the All-Ireland quarter-final.

The author Brian Carthy savours a quiet moment in the 'theatre of dreams'.

Poetry in motion. Tipperary's John Leahy shows how it should be done.

CLARE

BACK ROW L TO R: Brian Lohan, Michael O'Halloran, Brian Quinn, Ger O'Loughlin, Davy Fitzgerald, Colin Lynch, Barry Murphy, Conor Clancy, Seán McMahon;
FRONT ROW L TO R: Liam Doyle, David Forde, Anthony Daly, P.J. O'Connell, Jamesie O'Connor, Niall Gilligan.

KERRY

BACK ROW L TO R: Christy Walsh, Mike Casey, Tony Maunsell, Gary Frehill, John Healy, T.J. Curran, Willie Joe Leen, Gerry O'Sullivan, (Leo Griffin)
FRONT ROW L TO R: Ian Maunsell, Brendan O'Mahony, Mike Slattery, Padraig Cronin, John Foley, Ian Brick, Seán Fitzgerald.

SUNDAY, MAY 25, 1997

MUNSTER SENIOR HURLING CHAMPIONSHIP QUARTER-FINAL

LIMERICK versus WATERFORD

SEMPLE STADIUM, THURLES

REFEREE: SEANIE MC MAHON (CLARE)

RESULT: LIMERICK 2-20 WATERFORD 1-17

LIMERICK HURLERS ARE on the march again after a confident display against a young and inexperienced Waterford side that showed great character throughout. There was much to admire about Limerick's performance but their lapse of concentration in the closing stages somewhat diluted the positive manner of their victory.

Limerick were coasting to victory when they led by no less than eleven points just 15 minutes from time but appeared to drop their guard and allowed Waterford hit back with five unanswered points.

Waterford conceded far too many frees in the early stages but were still very much in contention until Barry Foley struck for two goals in a blistering four-minute spell that effectively ended the game as a contest. Limerick will rarely again get the 'rub of the green' that gifted them those two precious goals that turned the game so decisively in their favour. It proved a nightmare experience for Waterford goalkeeper, Ray Whitty. The first goal came about when Foley's shot caught Whitty by surprise and landed into the net for a tonic Limerick score. Four minutes later, Whitty failed to clear his lines and Foley was in like a flash to grab his second goal of the game. Shortly afterwards, the unfortunate Whitty was called ashore to be replaced by Brendan Landers.

Top scorer and key forward Paul Flynn replied with a Waterford goal to cut the arrears to six points after 27 minutes, but some solid freetaking by Gary Kirby left Limerick eight points clear at the interval on a 2-13 to 1-8 scoreline.

Waterford came back strongly in the early stages of the second-half and a point from Tony Browne was quickly followed by two more from Billy O'Sullivan to narrow the gap sufficiently to prompt Limerick manager, Tom Ryan, to make an inspired substitution. Ryan introduced Ciaran Carey and the captain showed no ill effects from an ankle injury with a superb display. Carey's arrival spurred Limerick on to greater effort and the Shannonsiders were rewarded with six unanswered points to effectively seal the issue.

Waterford applied the pressure in the closing fifteen minutes and scored five points without reply and would surely have got much closer but for the brilliance of Limerick goalkeeper, Albert Shanahan, who produced some superb saves.

SCORERS - LIMERICK: Barry Foley 2-1; Gary Kirby 0-6; Shane O'Neill 0-4; Mike Galligan 0-4; James Moran 0-3; T.J. Ryan 0-2
WATERFORD: Paul Flynn 1-7; Billy O'Sullivan 0-4; Tony Browne 0-3; Ken McGrath 0-2; Dave Bennett 0-1

LIMERICK

Albert Shanahan

Stephen McDonagh	Mike Nash	Declan Nash
Dave Clarke	Mark Foley	Ollie Moran
Mike Houlihan		Seán O'Neill
Mike Galligan	Gary Kirby	Barry Foley
James Moran	Shane O'Neill	T.J. Ryan

SUBSTITUTES: Ciaran Carey for Ollie Moran; Pat Heffernan for T.J. Ryan; John Flavin for Mark Foley

WATERFORD

Ray Whitty

Sean Cullinane	James O'Connor	Mark O'Sullivan
Stephen Frampton	Tom Feeney	Fergal Hartley
Tony Browne		Peter Queally
Paul Power	Ken McGrath	Dave Bennett
Billy O'Sullivan	Paul Flynn	Micheal White

SUBSTITUTES: Brendan Landers for Ray Whitty; Brian Green for Paul Power; Barry Walsh for Micheal White

LIMERICK
BACK ROW L TO R: T.J. Ryan, Mike Nash, Seán O'Neill, Gary Kirby, Shane O'Neill, James Moran, Ollie Moran, Dave Clarke; FRONT ROW L TO R: Declan Nash, Mike Houlihan, Barry Foley, Albert Shanahan, Mike Galligan, Stephen McDonagh, Mark Foley.

WATERFORD
BACK ROW L TO R: Tony Browne, Paul Power, Billy O'Sullivan, Stephen Frampton, Ken McGrath, Mark O'Sullivan, Paul Flynn, Peter Queally;
FRONT ROW L TO R: Tom Feeney, James O'Connor, Ray Whitty, Fergal Hartley, Seán Cullinane, Dave Bennett, Micheal White.

SUNDAY, JUNE 8, 1997

MUNSTER SENIOR HURLING CHAMPIONSHIP SEMI-FINAL

CLARE versus CORK

GAELIC GROUNDS, LIMERICK

REFEREE: PAT O'CONNOR (LIMERICK)

RESULT: CLARE 1-19 CORK 0-18

BRAVE CORK ARE on the way back but proud Clare go marching on! Cork hurlers restored their pride with a gutsy and skilful display that went a long way towards erasing the bitter disappointment of their 16 points drubbing by Limerick twelve months previously. That was a definite low point for Cork hurling but now the future looks much brighter after a vastly improved performance.

However, victory eluded Jimmy Barry Murphy's young team as Clare somehow found the character from deep within to withstand the onslaught. A late goal from Stephen McNamara served to bury Cork's dreams for another year at least. Clare manager Ger Loughnane was unable to conceal his delight when McNamara found the target. He was one happy man. Loughnane was devastated to lose to Limerick in 1996 after a spectacular injury-time point from Ciaran Carey and he was very relieved to see his team overcome the stubborn Cork challenge.

Clare led by just a single point at half-time after playing with the breeze, but

Loughnane, realising the urgent need for repair, introduced Stephen McNamara and David Forde in place of Niall Gilligan and Conor Clancy, and switched Ger 'Sparrow' O'Loughlin to full-forward. O'Loughlin prospered in his new role and produced a superb second-half display. His splendid point from play immediately after the re-start had the effect of lifting the Clare team. O'Loughlin scored a further two points during the next ten minutes and then provided the pass for McNamara's clinching goal. Furthermore, Clare's victory was built around inspirational defensive displays by full-back Brian Lohan and centre-half-back, Seán McMahon, both of whom thwarted many a Cork attack.

Clare began in confident fashion and, despite losing the injured Fergal Hegarty before the start, had moved 0-5 to 0-1 ahead after 12 minutes play. However, there were some positive signs for Cork early on and impressive corner-forward Joe Deane missed a chance of a goal. The quite brilliant Brian Corcoran was beginning to make a significant impact at centre-half-back and Seanie McGrath, who scored the opening point for Cork, was in sparkling form. Indeed, before the game had run its course, McGrath had proven himself to be a player of exceptional talent. He scored five points and was instrumental in the creation of many other Cork scores. His first touch was a revelation and he turned in a superb display. Although given much less room to showcase his skills in the second-half, McGrath was ever dangerous and scored three further points. Corcoran, for his part, had one of his best ever displays in a Cork jersey.

Three pointed frees from Jamesie O'Connor lifted the '95 All-Ireland Champions 0-8 to 0-3 ahead but a tremendous display by the Cork backs restricted the much vaunted Clare attack to just a single point in the closing fifteen minutes of the opening half. Cork stormed back and a point each from Ger Manley, Barry Egan, Deane, McGrath and Alan Browne ensured just one point separated the sides at the half-time interval.

O'Loughlin's move to full-forward after the re-start revitalised the Clare attack and his three early points against the breeze served to steady his colleagues. McMahon was strong and commanding at centre-half-back while Brian Lohan cleared his lines time and time again. Cork had their chances to win the game but the vital goal eluded them. Instead, McNamara latched on to a pass from O'Loughlin and crashed the ball to the Cork net. McGrath was deprived a goal in injury-time through a splendid save from Clare goalkeeper, Davy Fitzgerald.

SCORERS - CLARE: Jamesie O'Connor 0-6; Ger O'Loughlin 0-3; Seán McMahon 0-3; Stephen McNamara 1-0; Colin Lynch 0-2; Fergus Tuohy 0-2; Conor Clancy 0-1; David Forde 0-1; Anthony Daly 0-1;
CORK: Ger Manley 0-6; Seanie McGrath 0-5; Barry Egan 0-2; Joe Deane 0-2; Alan Browne 0-2; Alan Cummins 0-1

CLARE

	Davy Fitzgerald	
Michael O'Halloran	Brian Lohan	Frank Lohan
Liam Doyle	Sean McMahon	Anthony Daly
Ollie Baker		Colin Lynch
Fergus Tuohy	P.J. O'Connell	Jamesie O'Connor
Niall Gilligan	Conor Clancy	Ger O'Loughlin

SUBSTITUTES: Stephen McNamara for Niall Gilligan; David Forde for Conor Clancy; Andrew Whelan for O'Loughlin

CORK

Ger Cunningham

Fergal Ryan | John O'Driscoll | Diarmuid O'Sullivan

Sean Og O'hAilpin | Brian Corcoran | Timmy Kelleher

Fergal McCormack | Alan Cummins

Ger Manley | Kevin Murray | Barry Egan

Seanie McGrath | Alan Browne | Joe Deane

SUBSTITUTES: Mick Daly for Kevin Murray; Darren Ronan for Alan Cummins

CLARE

BACK ROW L TO R: Brian Lohan, Michael O'Halloran, Ger O'Loughlin, Conor Clancy, Colin Lynch, Davy Fitzgerald, Frank Lohan, Seán McMahon;

FRONT ROW L TO R: Fergus Tuohy, Liam Doyle, P.J. O'Connell, Anthony Daly, Ollie Baker, Jamesie O'Connor, Niall Gilligan.

CORK

BACK ROW L TO R: Ger Cunningham, Diarmuid O'Sullivan, Brian Corcoran, John O'Driscoll, Alan Cummins, Fergal McCormack, Alan Browne, Kevin Murray, Seán Og O'hAilpin;

FRONT ROW L TO R: Barry Egan, Timmy Kelleher, Seanie McGrath, Joe Deane, Fergal Ryan, Ger Manley.

SUNDAY, JUNE 15, 1997

MUNSTER SENIOR HURLING CHAMPIONSHIP SEMI-FINAL

TIPPERARY versus LIMERICK

SEMPLE STADIUM, THURLES

REFEREE: DICKIE MURPHY (WEXFORD)

RESULT: TIPPERARY 1-20 LIMERICK 0-13

THIS WAS A SWEET VICTORY for Tipperary. Limerick had recovered from a ten points half-time deficit to force a draw against Tipperary in last year's Munster Final and then won the replay by three points, but Tom Ryan's team found such heroics way beyond them for the second year running. Tipperary were determined to erase the memory of that defeat and how ironic it was that their winning margin this time round should be ten points.

The opening exchanges were keenly contested and the sides were level for the fifth time, 0-5 each, after 21 minutes play. All-Star Liam Cahill struck over the opening point inside half a minute but Gary Kirby was on the mark with the equalising point for Limerick soon afterwards. The scene was set! Both sides had periods of dominance in the first quarter but Limerick squandered a number of chances that should have yielded scores. Full-forward Shane O'Neill shot wide after being set up by Barry Foley, while Gary Kirby's attempted goal effort from a free was blocked by goalkeeper, Brendan Cummins. Tipperary had better luck. 'Man of the Match' Michael Cleary scored the only goal of the game after goalkeeper Joe Quaid blocked a powerful shot from John Leahy. Cleary kicked the loose ball past Cummins for a crucial goal. Opportunism at its very best!

Cleary continued to torment the Limerick defence and with Declan Ryan playing confidently at centre-half-forward, Tipperary went in at half-time 1-8 to 0-8 ahead. Mike Galligan, who was critical of the management for leaving him out of the starting fifteen, was introduced in place of Brian Tobin before half-time in an attempt to give the Limerick attack more direction and pace. Manager Tom Ryan also sent in Pat Heffernan at full-forward in place of Shane O'Neill at half-time. Limerick pressed hard for scores after the restart and Galligan sent over the opening point of the second-half to reduce the margin to just two points. Galligan played well throughout, but Tipperary continued to exert their influence through points from Kevin Tucker, Declan Ryan and Thomas Dunne. Leahy scored two further points to push Tipperary 1-13 to 0-10 clear after 50 minutes play.

Leahy and Ryan were easily two of the most influential players on the field. Both scored three points apiece and set up numerous other scores. Ciaran Carey's move to midfield failed to ignite Limerick's challenge. Inexplicably, the Shannonsiders faded rather badly in the closing quarter as Tipperary took control with fast, direct hurling. Limerick's fire had been doused and Tipperary reeled off points from Michael Cleary, Thomas Dunne, Liam Cahill, Declan Ryan, Philip O'Dwyer and Kevin Tucker. Tipperary outscored Limerick by 0-7 to 0-1 in the closing quarter to underline their dominance and secure a Munster Final meeting with Clare.

SCORERS - TIPPERARY: Michael Cleary 1-3; Thomas Dunne 0-5; Declan Ryan 0-3;

Kevin Tucker 0-3; John Leahy 0-3; Liam Cahill 0-2; Philip O'Dwyer 0-1
LIMERICK: Gary Kirby 0-5; Mike Houlihan 0-2; Mike Galligan 0-2; Dave Clarke 0-1; Mark Foley 0-1; Barry Foley 0-1; T.J. Ryan 0-1

TIPPERARY

Brendan Cummins

Paul Shelly — Noel Sheehy — Michael Ryan

Raymie Ryan — Colm Bonnar — Conor Gleeson

Aidan Butler — John Leahy

Kevin Tucker — Declan Ryan — Thomas Dunne

Liam Cahill — Michael Cleary — Philip O'Dwyer

SUBSTITUTES: Brendan Carroll for Aidan Butler;
Conal Bonnar for Raymie Ryan

LIMERICK

Joe Quaid

Stephen McDonagh — Mike Nash — Declan Nash

Dave Clarke — Ciaran Carey — Mark Foley

Mike Houlihan — Seán O'Neill

James Moran — Gary Kirby — Barry Foley

Brian Tobin — Shane O'Neill — T.J. Ryan

SUBSTITUTES: Mike Galligan for Brian Tobin;
Pat Heffernan for Shane O'Neill; Frankie Carroll for James Moran

TIPPERARY
BACK ROW L TO R: Raymie Ryan, Aidan Butler, Noel Sheehy, Michael Ryan, Conor Gleeson, Brendan Cummins, Thomas Dunne, Philip O'Dwyer;
FRONT ROW L TO R: Liam Cahill, Michael Cleary, John Leahy, Paul Shelly, Kevin Tucker, Colm Bonnar, Declan Ryan.

LIMERICK
BACK ROW L TO R: Mike Houlihan, T.J. Ryan, Barry Foley, Shane O'Neill, Seán O'Neill, Gary Kirby, Mike Nash, Dave Clarke; FRONT ROW L TO R: Brian Tobin, Declan Nash, Ciaran Carey, Stephen McDonagh, Joe Quaid, James Moran, Mark Foley.

SUNDAY, JULY 6, 1997

MUNSTER SENIOR HURLING CHAMPIONSHIP FINAL

CLARE versus TIPPERARY

PAIRC UÍ CHAOIMH

REFEREE: PAT O'CONNOR (LIMERICK)

RESULT: CLARE 1-18 TIPPERARY 0-18

FOR DECADES NOW, Clare hurlers have yearned to beat Tipperary on Munster Final day and their 1995 All-Ireland victory over Offaly served only to increase that desire rather than dilute it. When it was all over, only the scoreboard disguised Clare's superiority over a Tipperary team that played well below par. Yet only a puck of a ball separated the teams at the final whistle and furthermore, a late Tipperary onslaught almost yielded that levelling score. John Leahy fluffed a glorious chance of the equaliser when he mishit the ball completely from close range in injury-time.

It was Clare's first victory over Tipperary on Munster Final day and their supporters celebrated in a style that befitted such a unique occasion in the annals of hurling. Tipperary were devastated and the players and management found little solace in the loophole which allowed them back into the Championship as beaten provincial finalists. Clare had won the 1997 Munster Final and Tipperary were beaten. Simple and straightforward as that. Back-door entries were far from the thoughts of Tipperary folk on Sunday, July 6, 1997.

Defeat in a Munster Final has its own implications. Tipperary manager Len Gaynor spoke of 'Clare's fitness and the power of their running', while a deliriously happy Ger Loughnane made it clear the game was all about 'winning respect'.

Any doubts about the intensity of the desire of both sides to win this Munster Final, given the fact that the losers would still remain in the Championship, were soon dispelled. Munster Finals are for winning. Nothing less will suffice.

Tipperary led briefly early on by 0-2 to 0-1, but it soon became apparent that Clare had a distinct advantage in most sectors of the field. Clare were dominant in defence and midfield, with P.J. O'Connell, Jamesie O'Connor, Fergus Tuohy and Ger O'Loughlin very prominent in attack.

After the early exchanges, Clare took control and scored eight points without reply to move 0-10 to 0-2 ahead after 27 minutes. During that period, Philip O'Dwyer had an angled shot saved by the excellent Clare goalkeeper, Davy Fitzgerald, while All-Star Liam Cahill hit wide across the goal. Paul Shelly continued to play soundly in defence while goalkeeper, Brendan Cummins, was alert and assured between the Tipperary posts.

Trailing by eight points, Tipperary were in disarray, but the pattern of the game was changing. Thomas Dunne made a significant impact when moved to midfield in a switch with John Leahy, who prospered at wing-forward. The contributions of Dunne, Leahy and Declan Ryan sparked a revival in Tipperary's fortunes and the scores followed.

Leahy inspired his colleagues with two quite magnificent points from play.

Having failed to raise a flag for nearly twenty-three minutes, Tipperary scored six points in the closing nine minutes to trail by 0-13 to 0-8 at the interval. Clare hit ten wides in the first half and their five points lead hardly reflected their overall superiority. Barry Murphy came close to scoring a goal near the end of the first-half when he challenged Brendan Cummins.

Tipperary had played well below par in the first-half, but still found themselves in a reasonably healthy state at the break. Len Gaynor called Aidan Flanagan into action at the start of the second-half and he played his part as Tipperary whittled down Clare's lead. The battle was on in earnest. Now it was Clare's turn to feel the pressure and their defence committed some elementary mistakes just as Tipperary had done in the opening half.

Two points apiece from Thomas Dunne and Kevin Tucker and a splendid point from the ever-dangerous Declan Ryan tied the scores, 0-13 each, barely seven minutes after the re-start. But just when it appeared Clare were vulnerable, the pendulum swung back in their favour once again.

Sean McMahon landed a huge free. The confidence was soon back in Clare's play. Ollie Baker and Colin Lynch re-asserted themselves at midfield; Brian Lohan and Anthony Daly marshalled the defence, and Jamesie O'Connor raised his game to meet the challenge. Here is a player of real quality!

Substitute David Forde, who replaced Stephen McNamara, scored a point and then followed up with the only goal of the game to turn the tide saffron and blue once again. O'Connor rowed in with two more points to leave Clare in a very commanding position. Tipperary again clawed their way back and outscored Clare by 0-5 to 0-1 during the closing ten minutes and came tantalisingly close to securing a draw, but John Leahy failed to connect with the sliotar from close-range and the chance was lost. It was close at the finish for Clare, but in truth, their winning margin should have been greater. Times are changing!

SCORERS - CLARE: Jamesie O'Connor 0-5; David Forde 1-1; Ger O'Loughlin 0-3; Sean McMahon 0-3; P.J. O'Connell 0-2; Fergus Tuohy 0-1; Colin Lynch 0-1; Barry Murphy 0-1; Stephen McNamara 0-1
TIPPERARY: Thomas Dunne 0-7; Declan Ryan 0-4; John Leahy 0-3; Kevin Tucker 0-3; Michael Cleary 0-1

CLARE

Davy Fitzgerald

Michael O'Halloran · Brian Lohan · Frank Lohan

Liam Doyle · Sean McMahon · Anthony Daly

Ollie Baker · Colin Lynch

Jamesie O'Connor · Fergus Tuohy · P.J. O'Connell

Barry Murphy · Ger O'Loughlin · Stephen McNamara

SUBSTITUTES: David Forde for Stephen McNamara; Andrew Whelan for Barry Murphy; Conor Clancy for Andrew Whelan

TIPPERARY

Brendan Cummins

Paul Shelly · Noel Sheehy · Michael Ryan

Raymie Ryan · Colm Bonnar · Conor Gleeson

John Leahy · Aidan Butler

Kevin Tucker · Declan Ryan · Thomas Dunne

Liam Cahill · Michael Cleary · Philip O'Dwyer

SUBSTITUTES: Aidan Flanagan for Philip O'Dwyer; Conal Bonnar for Conor Gleeson

CLARE
BACK ROW L TO R: Brian Lohan, Michael O'Halloran, Colin Lynch, Stephen McNamara, Davy Fitzgerald, Frank Lohan, Ger O'Loughlin, Seán McMahon;
FRONT ROW L TO R: Barry Murphy, Liam Doyle, Ollie Baker, Anthony Daly, Jamesie O'Connor, Fergus Tuohy, P.J. O'Connell.

TIPPERARY
BACK ROW L TO R: Raymie Ryan, Philip O'Dwyer, Noel Sheehy, Conor Gleeson, Brendan Cummins, Thomas Dunne, Aidan Butler, Michael Ryan;
FRONT ROW L TO R: Liam Cahill, Michael Cleary, John Leahy, Paul Shelly, Kevin Tucker, Colm Bonnar, Declan Ryan.

SUNDAY, MAY 18, 1997

LEINSTER SENIOR HURLING CHAMPIONSHIP PRELIMINARY ROUND

DUBLIN versus WESTMEATH

CUSACK PARK, MULLINGAR

REFEREE: PAT DUNPHY (KILKENNY)

RESULT: DUBLIN 5-15 WESTMEATH 2-8

CORNER-FORWARD GERRY ENNIS scored an impressive 3-3 as Dublin registered the second highest score of the hurling Championship and in so doing, completely overwhelmed a disjointed Westmeath team by sixteen points on a 5-15 to 2-8 scoreline.

On a rain-sodden day at Cusack Park, Westmeath were simply out of their depth against a confident and highly motivated Dublin side determined to make an impression in their first foray into Championship '97. A lively and competitive opening quarter gave no indication of what was about to unfold as Westmeath more than held their own with some positive and direct hurling which yielded a point each from Seán McLoughlin and Barry Kennedy to leave the sides on level terms.

And then it all began to go terribly wrong for the Midlanders! Eamonn Morrissey turned the game with a touch of genius that brightened a dull afternoon at Cusack Park.

The former Kilkenny star gathered the ball and moved past two defenders before rifling an unstoppable shot to the roof of the net.

The goal transformed Dublin and thereafter the result was never in doubt as Westmeath fell asunder under the intense pressure applied by such stars as Ennis, Morrissey and Jamesie 'Shiner' Brennan. All three made valuable contributions as Dublin grew in confidence and powered on to an easy victory. 'Man Of The Match' Ennis scored the first of his three goals when he kicked the ball to the net after 30 minutes and the Craobh Chiarain sharpshooter heaped further misery on a beleaguered Westmeath back-line with his second goal barely thirty seconds into the second-half.

Although Seán McLoughlin gave Westmeath supporters a brief glimmer of hope when he crashed the ball to the net from a free after 39 minutes, it was all hopelessly downhill for the Midlanders from there on, as Dublin took complete control.

Ennis and Brian McMahon scored a goal each inside a minute midway through the second-half to push the rampant Dubs some twenty points clear. Substitute Pat Clarke scored a Westmeath goal near the finish, but by that late stage, Dublin had their day's work complete and were eagerly anticipating a Leinster semi-final showdown with Kilkenny.

Dublin manager Michael O'Grady had good reason to be well satisfied with the way his team performed in difficult conditions.

"Even though we had a one-hundred-percent record going into the game, we were still very apprehensive. Dublin hadn't won a first round Championship game in five years, so we had no reason to feel cocky. We started slowly enough and Westmeath pressurised us a lot and an early goal for them could have damaged us. Eventually, we found the target and pulled away easily. Gerry Ennis had a great day scoring 3-3 and Liam Walsh was outstanding at wing back."

SCORERS - DUBLIN: Gerry Ennis 3-3; Jamesie Brennan 0-6; Eamonn Morrissey 1-2; Brian McMahon 1 0; Liam Walsh 0-1; Shane Dalton 0-1; Conor McCann 0-1; Stephen Perkins 0-1
WESTMEATH: Seán McLoughlin 1-3; Pat Clarke 1-0; Robbie Galvin 0-2; Barry Kennedy 0-1; Derek Gallagher 0-1; Pat Connaughton 0-1

DUBLIN

Brendan McLoughlin

John Finnegan — Sean Power — Sean Duignan
Liam Walsh — Peter Brady — Ruairi Boland

Jamesie Brennan — Barry O'Sullivan

Conor McCann — Brian McMahon — Stephen Perkins
Eamonn Morrissey — Shane Dalton — Gerry Ennis

SUBSTITUTES. Paul O'Donoghue for Jamesie Brennan; Simon Byrne for Brian McMahon; Philip Harney for Ruairí Boland

WESTMEATH

Seamus Lynch

Ollie Devine | Peter Dalton | Brendan Williams

Darren McCormack | Christo Murtagh | Derek Gallagher

Seamus Reilly | Robbie Galvin

Francis O'Farrell | Sean McLoughlin | Alfie Devine

Barry Kennedy | Pat Connaughton | Paul Williams

SUBSTITUTES: Pat Clarke for Francis O'Farrell; Seamus Qualter for Pat Connaughton; Fergal Fagan for Paul Williams

DUBLIN
BACK ROW L TO R: Gerry Ennis, Eamonn Morrissey, Stephen Perkins, Barry O'Sullivan, Conor McCann, Liam Walsh, Shane Dalton, Seán Duignan,
FRONT ROW L TO : Seán Power, Peter Brady, Brendan McLoughlin, Brian McMahon, Jamesie Brennan, Ruairi Boland, John Finnegan.

WESTMEATH
BACK ROW L TO R: Seán McLoughlin, Brendan Williams, Christo Murtagh, Francis O'Farrell, Seamus Reilly, Pat Connaughton, Darren McCormack, Peter Dalton;
FRONT ROW L TO R: Paul Williams, Alfie Devine, Barry Kennedy, Robbie Galvin, Ollie Devine, Seamus Lynch, Derek Gallagher.

SUNDAY, MAY 18, 1997

LEINSTER SENIOR HURLING CHAMPIONSHIP PRELIMINARY ROUND

OFFALY versus MEATH

CUSACK PARK, MULLINGAR

REFEREE: PADDY NEARY (KILKENNY)

RESULT: OFFALY 3-20 MEATH 0-8

JOHNNY DOOLEY was the scoring hero as Offaly coasted to an impressive twenty points victory in an all-too-one-sided game in atrocious weather conditions at Cusack Park.

The Seir Kieran marksman made light of the inclement weather and had scored 1-9 by the time manager John McIntyre decided to call him ashore late in the game. The beleaguered Meath defence were mightily relieved to see Dooley take his leave of the action, but there was little respite as his replacement, Gary Cahill, scored a goal on the stroke of full-time to complete the rout.

It was a profitable day all round for the Dooleys! Apart from Johnny's 1-9 contribution, Billy scored 0-2 while eldest brother, Joe, accounted for 1-2 of Offaly's total.

Overwhelming favourites Offaly, given a stern test by Meath in last year's Championship before eventually winning by six points, controlled matters from the start this time round and their total dominance became more and more evident as the game progressed.

Offaly have often been criticised for allowing the opposition back into the game, but there was absolutely no sign of complacency on this occasion. Clearly, manager McIntyre had hammered home his message in the weeks leading up to the game and the players had taken cognizance of what he had to say.

Meath won a fair share of possession in the early stages, but a point each from Martin Massey and Pat Potterton was their only tangible reward after some 14 minutes play, by which time Offaly had amassed five points. Offaly's opening point came from Paudie Mulhare after three minutes play, but the St. Rynaghs' clubman had to retire soon afterwards because of a facial injury.

Joe Dooley turned the game decisively in Offaly's favour with the opening goal on 20 minutes after good work by Joe Erritty. Two points from Pat Potterton and one from Benny Murray kept Meath in touch until Johnny Dooley fired home Offaly's second goal four minutes before the break to leave his side 2-8 to 0-5 ahead at the interval.

Meath's best forwards, Pat Potterton and Mike Cole, scored a point each shortly after the re-start, but to no avail as Offaly powered full steam ahead. Johnny Dooley shot over the bar from a penalty and there was no let-up as he continued to torment the Meath back line with superb points from both play and frees.

Offaly outscored a disappointing Meath side by 1-12 to 0-3 in the second-half to underline their superiority and issue a warning to quarter-final opponents, Laois.

SCORERS - OFFALY: Johnny Dooley 1-9; Joe Dooley 1-2; Killian Farrell 0-4; Gary Cahill 1-0; Billy Dooley 0-2; Johnny Pilkington 0-2; Paudie Mulhare 0-1
MEATH: Pat Potterton 0-4; Mike Cole 0-2; Benny Murray 0-1; Martin Massey 0-1

OFFALY

David Hughes

Hubert Rigney — Kevin Kinahan — Martin Hanamy

Brian Whelahan — Kevin Martin — Colm Cassidy

Johnny Pilkington — Ger Oakley

Johnny Dooley — Paudie Mulhare — Killian Farrell

Billy Dooley — Joe Erritty — Joe Dooley

SUBSTITUTES: Michael Duignan for Paudie Mulhare; John Troy for Ger Oakley; Gary Cahill for Johnny Dooley

MEATH

Mark Gannon

Anton O'Neill — Paddy Kelly — Charlie Keenan

Nicky Horan — Declan Murray — Sean Kealy

Paul Donnelly — Brian Gilsennan

Martin Massey — Martin Smith — Fergus McMahon

Pat Potterton — Mike Cole — Benny Murray

SUBSTITUTES: P.J. Walsh for Brian Gilsennan

OFFALY

BACK ROW L TO R: Johnny Pilkington, Hubert Rigney, Kevin Kinahan, Ger Oakley, David Hughes, Joe Erritty, Kevin Martin, Brian Whelahan;

FRONT ROW L TO R: Billy Dooley, Paudie Mulhare, Killian Farrell, Martin Hanamy, Joe Dooley, Colm Cassidy, Johnny Dooley.

MEATH
BACK ROW L TO R: Declan Murray, Brian Gilsenan, Paul Donnelly, Martin Massey, Martin Smith, Benny Murray, Nicky Horan, Anton O'Neill;
FRONT ROW L TO R: Charlie Keenan, Seán Kealy, Pat Potterton, Mark Gannon, Paddy Kelly, Mickey Cole, Fergal McMahon.

SUNDAY, JUNE 8, 1997

LEINSTER SENIOR HURLING CHAMPIONSHIP QUARTER-FINAL

OFFALY versus LAOIS

CROKE PARK

REFEREE: DICKIE MURPHY (WEXFORD)

RESULT: OFFALY 1-11 LAOIS 2-7

RANK OUTSIDERS LAOIS tore the formbook to shreds with an astonishing second-half comeback that surely deserved a better result than an agonising one point defeat.

A thumbnail sketch of the game reveals that Offaly led by three points at the end of a dire first-half and, having extended their lead to seven points midway through the second-half, appeared on course for a comfortable victory. Then P.J. Peacock scored a goal to spark a Laois revival and with substitutes Tony Dunne and Joe Dollard leading the charge, Babs Keating's team whittled the lead down to a single point as ragged Offaly held on for dear life.

Underdogs Laois, who had an appalling League campaign, deserved at least a draw, but paid dearly for some bad wides near the finish of what was a poor game until Peacock made that telling contribution with a finely taken goal. Tony Dunne, who replaced Noel Delaney at half-time, turned in a superlative display of non-stop hurling and was instrumental in Laois producing such a storming finish. Offaly played well below par and the old failings manifested themselves again with near disastrous consequences.

The quality of fare on offer in the opening twenty minutes was less than mediocre as both sets of players, with few exceptions, continually laboured with even the most elementary facets of the game. The sides were level 0-2 apiece after nineteen minutes of moderate play when Owen Coss put Laois ahead for the second and last time with a goal that exposed glaring weaknesses in the Offaly defence. Offaly hit back with a vengeance and Joe Erritty scored a superb goal which was followed by a point from play by Joe Dooley and two more from frees by brother, Johnny.

Offaly led at the interval by 1-5 to 1-2, thanks mainly to the contributions of Kevin Martin, Brian Whelahan, Michael Duignan and free-taker, Johnny Dooley.

The standard of hurling improved somewhat in the second-half and David Hughes had to produce a brilliant save to deny Owen Coss a certain goal just five minutes after the re-start. Offaly took advantage of that let-off and a point each from Johnny Dooley, Johnny Pilkington, Michael Duignan and Gary Cahill pushed the Faithful County seven points clear.

But urged on by goalkeeper, Ricky Cashin, defenders Niall Rigney and Paul Cuddy and substitutes, Tony Dunne and Joe Dollard, Laois bravely set about retrieving the game.

Peacock's goal started the onslaught; Joe Dooley steadied Offaly nerves with a point; Dollard converted two frees; impressive Seamus Cuddy whipped over a point from play and Laois sensed victory when Peacock sent over his second point to reduce the margin to the minimum. Laois were now swarming all over a disjointed Offaly side, but the equalising point never arrived due to poor marksmanship and some frantic defending by the Offaly backline.

Offaly manager John McIntyre was none too pleased with his team's lethargic performance and their final quarter fade-out that nearly cost them the game.

"I died a thousand deaths on the sideline and I think we had nine lives on the playing field," John said. "We treated Laois with every respect as we knew we had to be on our guard today. Laois had a bad League campaign but we knew there had to be a kick in them somewhere and we were expecting it today. We didn't underestimate them."

SCORERS - OFFALY: Johnny Dooley 0-5; Joe Erritty 1-0; Joe Dooley 0-2; Michael Duignan 0-2; Gary Cahill 0-1; Johnny Pilkington 0-1
LAOIS: P.J. Peacock 1-2; Owen Coss 1-0; Joe Dollard 0-2; Seamus Cuddy 0-1; Tony Dunne 0-1; Bill Maher 0-1

OFFALY

David Hughes

Hubert Rigney — Kevin Kinahan — Martin Hanamy

Brian Whelahan — Kevin Martin — Colm Cassidy

Johnny Pilkington — Michael Duignan

Johnny Dooley — Paudie Mulhare — Killian Farrell

Billy Dooley — Joe Erritty — Joe Dooley

SUBSTITUTES: Gary Cahill for Killian Farrell;
John Troy for Billy Dooley; Gary Hannify for Paudie Mulhare

LAOIS

Ricky Cashin

John Shorthall | Cyril Duggan | John Taylor

Niall Rigney | Paul Cuddy | Seamus Dooley

David Cuddy | Declan Conroy

P.J. Peacock | Seamus Cuddy | Fionan O'Sullivan

Noel Delaney | Owen Coss | Bill Maher

SUBSTITUTES: Tony Dunne for Noel Delaney;
Joe Dollard for Fionan O'Sullivan; Tomas Kenna for Declan Conroy

OFFALY
BACK ROW L TO R: Johnny Pilkington, Michael Duignan, David Hughes, Hubert Rigney, Kevin Martin, Kevin Kinahan, Joe Erritty, Brian Whelahan;
FRONT ROW L TO R: Paudie Mulhare, Billy Dooley, Killian Farrell, Martin Hanamy, Joe Dooley, Colm Cassidy, Johnny Dooley.

LAOIS
BACK ROW L TO R: Niall Rigney, David Cuddy, Owen Coss, Seamus Cuddy, Cyril Duggan, Declan Conroy, Bill Maher;
FRONT ROW L TO R: Fionain O'Sullivan, Seamus Dooley, Paul Cuddy, Ricky Cashin, P.J. Peacock, John Shorthall, John Taylor, Noel Delaney.

SUNDAY, JUNE 22, 1997

LEINSTER SENIOR HURLING CHAMPIONSHIP SEMI-FINAL

KILKENNY versus DUBLIN

CROKE PARK

REFEREE: PAT AHEARNE (CARLOW)

RESULT: KILKENNY 2-20 DUBLIN 2-13

TWO FLASHES OF brilliance and the Dublin hurlers were out of Championship '97! The Dubs were holding on to a slender one point lead entering the final ten minutes when substitute P.J Delaney gathered the ball and struck an angled shot to the net; a minute later, DJ Carey outfielded Ruairi Boland to score a stunning goal.

To compound their misfortune, Dublin were reduced to fourteen players when full-back, Seán Power, was dismissed for a second bookable offence after 64 minutes and shortly afterwards, Eamon Morrissey's powerfully struck shot was deflected over the crossbar by goalkeeper Adrian Ronan.

Kilkenny's revival was due in no small part to substitute Philip Larkin who made a very considerable impact at midfield when introduced in place of Aidan Lawlor at the half-time interval. Larkin had an outstanding game and his display, together with the contribution of another substitute, P.J. Delaney, helped pave the way for a Kilkenny victory.

As always, DJ Carey played a key role and his tally of 1-7 once again underlined his immense talent and his importance to Kilkenny. The Gowran star scored two points in the opening nine minutes as Kilkenny confidently moved 0-5 to 0-1 ahead, but former Kilkenny player Jamesie Brennan steadied the 'Dubs' with two points before edging them in front for the first time with a goal. Brennan's long-range free went over the head of goalkeeper, Adrian Ronan, and into the net for a tonic goal that reversed the earlier trend.

Shortly afterwards, play was held up for a considerable length of time to allow an overflow of supporters from the New Stand cross to the Hogan Stand. Dublin refused to be sidetracked by off-field activities and with Jamesie Brennan continuing to dictate the pace, Michael O'Grady's highly-motivated team more than shaded the exchanges.

Conor McCann and Stephen Perkins were prominent in the attack and with Brennan finding the range, Dublin still held on to a two points advantage approaching half-time.

Their cause received a considerable boost just before the interval when Gerry Ennis, scorer of 3-3 against Westmeath in the previous round, struck for a superb goal to push Dublin 2-8 to 0-9 ahead at half-time.

Unperturbed, Kilkenny started the second-half in confident fashion with a point apiece from Charlie Carter and DJ Carey. Kilkenny appeared to be capable of lifting their game when required but found Dublin in no mood to capitulate. Jamesie Brennan and Eamonn Morrissey continued to keep the pressure on Kilkenny but the tide was turning a distinct shade of 'black and amber'and by the time John Costello converted his third long-range free, the Cats had reduced the deficit to just two points.

Dublin were still holding on grimly as the game entered the final ten minutes but first

Delaney and then Carey struck for a goal; Dublin full-back Seán Power was sent off and Kilkenny goalkeeper, Adrian Ronan, deflected an Eamonn Morrissey penalty over the bar. The Kilkenny Cats were still alive, and the Dubs would have to wait another year at least for Championship glory.

Some weeks later Dublin manager, Michael O'Grady, whose mother sadly died on the Saturday night before the game, reflected on the defeat.

"We started the game slowly and fell four points behind in the early stages. Our backs seemed nervous and their striking was poor in parts. Once we got our first point, we began to move a bit better and Jamesie Brennan's goal really lifted the team," Michael says. "Shortly after this, the referee had to stop the game due to the overcrowding in the Cusack Stand. It was a strange sensation standing on the line watching it. However, the Dubs fans on the Hill were very vocal and some people feel that this stoppage affected us more than Kilkenny. I'm not really sure. We continued to play well and continued to lead by five points at half-time. I felt we needed to dominate the early part of the second-half, but we failed to do so and Kilkenny clawed their way back. Philip Larkin was playing well at midfield and we found it difficult to find our share in the second-half. P.J. Delaney got a rather lucky goal and DJ Carey came from nowhere to score a brilliant second just two minutes later. We still battled on and did a lot of attacking right up to the end."

KILKENNY: DJ Carey 1-7; P.J. Delaney 1-0; Charlie Carter 0-3; John Costello 0-3; Philip Larkin 0-2; Andy Comerford 0-2; Michael Phelan 0-1; Peter Barry 0-1; Niall Moloney 0-1;
DUBLIN: Jamesie Brennan 1-8; Eamonn Morrissey 0-3; Gerry Ennis 1-0; Conor McCann 0-2

KILKENNY

	Adrian Ronan	
Eddie O'Connor	Pat O'Neill	Willie O'Connor
Liam Keoghan	Dan O'Neill	John Costello
Andy Comerford		Aidan Lawlor
Brian McEvoy	Canice Brennan	Peter Barry
Niall Moloney	DJ Carey	Charlie Carter

SUBSTITUTES: Philip Larkin for Aidan Lawlor; Michael Phelan for Canice Brennan; P.J. Delaney for Niall Moloney

DUBLIN

	Brendan McLoughlin	
John Finnegan	Sean Power	Andy O'Callaghan
Sean Duignan	Paddy Brady	Ruairi Boland
Jamesie Brennan		Barry O'Sullivan
Conor McCann	Stephen Perkins	Brian McMahon
Eamonn Morrissey	Colin Featherstone	Gerry Ennis

SUBSTITUTES: Mick Morrissey for Barry O'Sullivan; Paul O'Donoghue for Colin Featherstone; Philip Harney for Seán Duignan

KILKENNY
BACK ROW L TO R: Dan O'Neill, Andy Comerford, Canice Brennan, Niall Moloney, Aidan Lawlor, John Costello, Peter Barry, Pat O'Neill;
FRONT ROW L TO R: Liam Keoghan, Charlie Carter, DJ Carey, Brian McEvoy, Adrian Ronan, Willie O'Connor, Eddie O'Connor.

DUBLIN
BACK ROW L TO R: John Finnegan, Stephen Perkins, Barry O'Sullivan, Colin Featherstone, Peter Brady, Eamonn Morrissey, Seán Duignan;
FRONT ROW L TO R: Jamesie Brennan, Gerry Ennis, Conor McCann, Brian McMahon, Brendan McLoughlin, Seán Power, Ruairi Boland, Andy O'Callaghan.

SUNDAY, JUNE 22, 1997

LEINSTER SENIOR HURLING CHAMPIONSHIP SEMI-FINAL

WEXFORD versus OFFALY

CROKE PARK

REFEREE: AODAIN MAC SUIBHNE (DUBLIN)

RESULT: WEXFORD 3-12 OFFALY 2-12

DAMIEN FITZHENRY was the toast of Wexford after pulling off a spectacular injury-time save from Billy Dooley to consign Offaly to Championship also-rans. Corner-forward Dooley looked odds-on to score the equalising goal, but his powerful shot was blocked and cleared to safety by Fitzhenry. It was a close call for Wexford who were under extreme pressure to deliver after all the hype that surrounded last year's heroics which yielded them a first All-Ireland title in twenty-eight years.

Offaly, who conceded two easy first-half goals, turned the game around in the last quarter only to be denied a draw by the outstanding Duffry Rovers goalkeeper.

Last year's All-Star and 'Hurler Of The Year', Martin Storey displayed his tremendous leadership qualities at centre-half-forward, particularly in the closing stages when Offaly found new life and began to slowly claw their way back into the game. The confidence that comes from winning an All-Ireland was evident in Wexford's play and they dominated in several key areas. It was a personal triumph for Storey who was thrilled with his own performance.

"A lot of people said to me that I should have left it after last year's All-Ireland and go out in a blaze of glory as captain and 'Hurler Of The Year', but I was determined to prove I could still do it. I was happy with the way everything worked out."

Wexford had many heroes on the day; Ger Cush was outstanding at full-back and his defensive colleagues were very effective, with Eugene Furlong and Rod Guiney particularly prominent.

Wexford set about their task with confidence and vigour and, to coincide with a downpour, Liam Dunne struck a '65 which went over the head of Offaly goalkeeper David Hughes and into the net. Wexford continued to press home their advantage and Garry Laffan scored his first goal after another mistake by goalkeeper Hughes to push the All-Ireland Champions eight points clear.

Laffan scored his second goal two minutes before the break when he struck an overhead shot to the net, but Billy Dooley scored an excellent goal to give Offaly renewed hope for the start of the second-half.

Wexford led at half-time by 3-6 to 1-6 but with Brian Whelahan, midfielder Johnny Pilkington and forwards Billy and Johnny Dooley making inroads, Offaly began to exert their influence. However, poor finishing militated against the 1994 All-Ireland Champions and Wexford had moved seven points clear with less than a quarter of an hour remaining. But then came the best score of the game!

Pilkington rounded off a great run from midfield down the centre with a spectacular goal to set the game alight. Johnny Dooley scored a point six minutes later to leave the game in the balance entering the final five minutes. Wexford held on mainly due to solid defending and valuable contributions from substitute Rory McCarthy and the highly impressive Storey, who struck over his fourth point from play in injury-time.

Then came that marvellous save by Fitzhenry and the All-Ireland Champions had survived. But only just!

SCORERS - WEXFORD: Gary Laffan 2-0; Martin Storey 0-4; Tom Dempsey 0-4; Liam Dunne 1-0; Paul Codd 0-1; Rory McCarthy 0-1; Larry Murphy 0-2
OFFALY: Johnny Dooley 0-7; Johnny Pilkington 1-1; Billy Dooley 1-0; Michael Duignan 0-2; Ger Oakley 0-1; Colm Cassidy 0-1

WEXFORD

Damien Fitzhenry

Colm Kehoe — Ger Cush — Eugene Furlong
Rod Guiney — Liam Dunne — Sean Flood
Larry O'Gorman — Adrian Fenlon
Michael Jordan — Martin Storey — Larry Murphy
Paul Codd — Gary Laffan — Tom Dempsey

SUBSTITUTES: Rory McCarthy for Michael Jordan;
Billy Byrne for Paul Codd; Eamonn Scallan for Larry Murphy

OFFALY

David Hughes

Hubert Rigney — Kevin Kinahan — Martin Hanamy
Brian Whelahan — Kevin Martin — Colm Cassidy
Johnny Pilkington — Michael Duignan
Johnny Dooley — Joe Erritty — Joe Dooley
Billy Dooley — Gary Hannify — John Troy

SUBSTITUTES: Gary Cahill for Gary Hannify;
Ger Oakley for Joe Dooley; Killian Farrell for John Troy

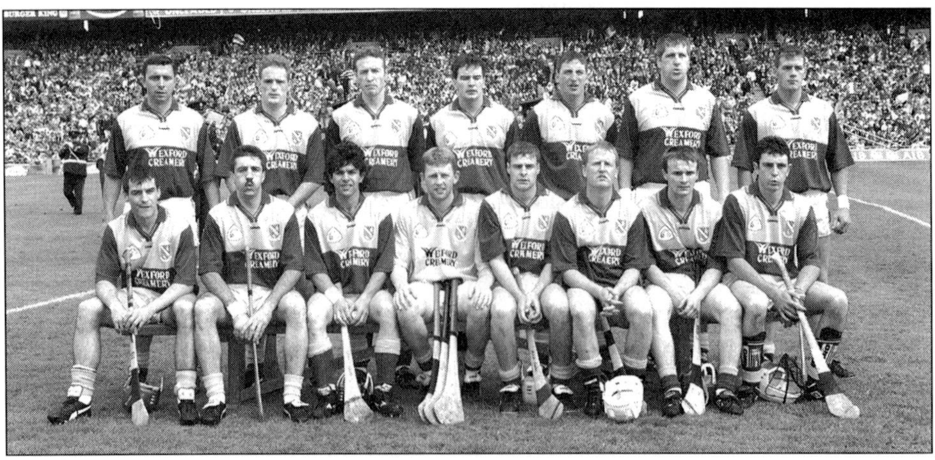

WEXFORD
BACK ROW L TO R: Larry O'Gorman, Rod Guiney, Larry Murphy, Adrian Fenlon, Gary Laffan, Ger Cush, Eugene Furlong;
FRONT ROW L TO R: Liam Dunne, Martin Storey, Seán Flood, Damien Fitzhenry, Micheal Jordan, Tom Dempsey, Colm Kehoe, Paul Codd.

OFFALY
BACK ROW L TO R: Kevin Kinahan, Hubert Rigney, Gary Hanniffy, David Hughes, Johnny Pilkington, Joe Erritty, Michael Duignan, Brian Whelahan;
FRONT ROW L TO R: Billy Dooley, Martin Hanamy, John Troy, Joe Dooley, Colm Cassidy, Kevin Martin, Johnny Dooley.

SUNDAY, JULY 13, 1997

LEINSTER SENIOR HURLING CHAMPIONSHIP FINAL

WEXFORD versus KILKENNY

CROKE PARK

REFEREE: AODAIN MAC SUIBHNE (DUBLIN)

RESULT: WEXFORD 2-14 KILKENNY 1-11

A GAME TO REMEMBER! The passion, skill, speed and sheer physical endeavour of the exchanges were the hallmarks of this riveting Leinster Championship Final between age-old rivals Wexford and Kilkenny. It was a highly physical encounter, even at times over-robust, as players from both sides gave their all in pursuit of victory. The game took a while to gain momentum but gradually picked up pace and finished in a welter of excitement. Super-sub Billy Byrne turned the game decisively in favour of the All-Ireland Champions with a smash-and-grab 1-2 in the seven pulsating minutes he was on the field. Stuff of dreams for 37-year-old Billy, a hurling man to his fingertips. He knew the hard times in the purple and gold jersey, but last year's All-Ireland victory more than made amends for all the heartbreak around the hurling fields of Leinster. And now this! Stuff of dreams, sure enough!

An injury-time goal from P.J. Delaney helped Kilkenny to a five points lead at the half-time interval and the game was in the balance until veteran Billy Byrne made his entrance. With his first touch after about ten seconds, Billy kicked the sliotar to the Kilkenny net. Thereafter there was no stopping the Naomh Eanna player and he landed two more points to inspire Wexford and deny Kilkenny a victory that looked a real possibility entering the final ten minutes.

Kilkenny made their intentions clear early on and by the 21st minute had moved 0-6 to 0-2 ahead with no less than five forwards having found the range. Kilkenny looked assured and confident while the All-Ireland Champions were struggling in some key areas. That sustained period of Kilkenny pressure soon abated and Wexford rallied with a point each from Paul Codd, Tom Dempsey and Gary Laffan.

Kilkenny battled back with a point from Philip Larkin and a somewhat fortuitous goal from P.J. Delaney. Larry O'Gorman's poorly hit crossfield pass was mis-hit by Peter Barry and missed completely by Eugene Furlong before Delaney took full advantage of the comedy of errors to crash the ball home.

Delaney's goal and the fact that Ger Cush had to retire injured at half-time represented a huge blow to Wexford and it looked bleak when Andy Comerford stretched Kilkenny's lead with a fine point after the re-start.

Kilkenny lost influential corner-back Eddie O'Connor through injury and very soon the tide turned when Tom Dempsey scored a Wexford goal to reduce the margin to just three points. Wexford's play improved considerably after the goal and their defence continually closed down the Kilkenny forward line. Liam Dunne at centre-half-back, midfielder Adrian Fenlon and wing-forward Rory McCarthy performed magnificently as Wexford's comeback gained momentum.

The Kilkenny defence looked steady enough and their strong resistance ensured Wexford had to work extremely hard to get scores. The All-Ireland Champions went ahead for the very first time after 59 minutes through a Paul Codd free but almost immediately Charlie Carter replied with a point for Kilkenny to level the game.

The energetic and highly skilful Rory McCarthy edged Wexford ahead again with a fine point before substitute Billy Byrne cut loose and wrapped up the game literally seconds after coming on to the field.

SCORERS - WEXFORD: Billy Byrne 1-2; Rory McCarthy 0-4; Tom Dempsey 1-1; Paul Codd 0-3; Gary Laffan 0-2; Larry Murphy 0-1; Martin Storey 0-1
KILKENNY: P.J. Delaney 1-1; Charlie Carter 0-3; Peter Barry 0-3; DJ Carey 0-1; Philip Larkin 0-1; Andy Comerford 0-1; Niall Maloney 0-1

WEXFORD

Damien Fitzhenry

Colm Kehoe — Ger Cush — Eugene Furlong
Rod Guiney — Liam Dunne — Sean Flood
Larry O'Gorman — Adrian Fenlon
Rory McCarthy — Martin Storey — Larry Murphy
Paul Codd — Gary Laffan — Tom Dempsey

SUBSTITUTES: Dave Guiney for Ger Cush; Billy Byrne for Larry Murphy

KILKENNY

Joe Dermody

Eddie O'Connor — Pat O'Neill — Willie O'Connor

Dan O'Neill — Liam Keoghan — John Costello

Philip Larkin — Andy Comerford

Peter Barry — John Power — DJ Carey

Niall Maloney — P.J. Delaney — Charlie Carter

SUBSTITUTES: David Beirne for Eddie O'Connor; Denis Byrne for Niall Maloney; Michael Phelan for John Power

WEXFORD
BACK ROW L TO R: Larry O'Gorman, Rod Guiney, Eugene Furlong, Adrian Fenlon, Larry Murphy, Gary Laffan, Ger Cush; FRONT ROW L TO R: Liam Dunne, Tom Dempsey, Martin Storey, Damien Fitzhenry, Seán Flood, Paul Codd, Colm Kehoe, Rory McCarthy.

KILKENNY
BACK ROW L TO R: Philip Larkin, John Power, Andy Comerford, Niall Moloney, John Costello, Peter Barry, Pat O'Neill; FRONT ROW L TO R: Eddie O'Connor, Liam Keoghan, Charlie Carter, Joe Dermody, DJ Carey, P.J. Delaney, Dan O'Neill, Willie O'Connor.

SATURDAY, JULY 12, 1997

CONNACHT SENIOR HURLING FINAL

GALWAY versus ROSCOMMON

ATHLEAGUE

REFEREE: PAT O'CONNOR (LIMERICK)

RESULT: GALWAY 6-24 ROSCOMMON 0-5

THERE WAS NOTHING to be learned and even less to be gained by playing this fixture which was revived in 1995 after a gap of 73 years. Roscommon were completely out of their depth and the game itself will be remembered above all else for the serious head injury sustained by Galway full-forward, Joe Rabbitte, early in the second-half. Rabbitte lay unconscious on the pitch for nearly eleven minutes before being transferred by ambulance to Roscommon hospital. Roscommon full-back, Padraig Feeney, was sent-off for his involvement in the incident that led to Rabbitte's injury.

Roscommon were forced to line-out without a number of their key players, and the withdrawal of centre-half-back Mickey Feeney just before the start further depleted their struggling team.

Galway's winning margin of 37 points was by far the biggest of the 1997 Hurling and Football Championships. Furthermore, their total of 6-24 was the highest score recorded in the Championship, while Roscommon's total of 0-5 was the lowest.

Senior Championship debutant, Alan Kerins, scored 3-2 in the opening half while teenager Eugene Cloonan added 0-6 as Galway coasted to a 3-15 to 0-4 half-time lead. Roscommon completely capitulated in the second quarter as a far superior Galway side produced exhibition hurling and the margin at the interval could have been even greater but for some fine saves by Roscommon goalkeeper, Adrian Tully.

One of the highpoints of the first-half was a truly splendid point from a side-line cut by Roscommon wing-forward, Brendan Boyle, a member of the Athleague club. Colm Kelly proved more than a match for Michael Healy when he moved to centre-half-forward before the midway point of the first-half.

Joe Rabbitte made his contribution by scoring a goal some four minutes after the restart to stretch Galway's lead to a staggering 25 points, 4-17 to 0-4. Shortly afterwards, the Athenry club man was knocked unconscious and, as Cyril Farrell said later: "When a player is out cold for ten minutes, it puts everything into perspective. We all have to go to work on Monday morning."

A goal each from Eugene Cloonan and Francis Forde further demoralised an outclassed Roscommon side that could only manage a single point in the second-half. I must say, I have great admiration for Michael Kelly, Johnny Haughey and Tommy Healy, and the many other hard working officials who strive to promote the game of hurling in Roscommon. Their dedication and commitment to the ancient game deserves to be recognised.

SCORERS - GALWAY: Alan Kerins 3-2; Eugene Cloonan 1-7; Francis Forde 1-2; Justin Campbell 0-4; Joe McGrath 0-4; Joe Rabbitte 1-1; Vinny Maher 0-2; Darragh Coen 0-1; Kevin Broderick 0-1; ROSCOMMON: Colm Kelly 0-2; Brendan Boyle 0-2; Liam Murray 0-1

GALWAY

Pat Costello

Tom Helebert	William Burke	Brian Feeney
Nigel Shaughnessy	Michael Healy	Cathal Moore
Joe Cooney		Vinnie Maher
Justin Campbell	Joe McGrath	Kevin Broderick
Alan Kerins	Joe Rabbitte	Eugene Cloonan

SUBSTITUTES: Francis Forde for Joe Rabbitte; Darragh Coen for Eugene Cloonan

ROSCOMMON

Adrian Tully

Marty Healy	Padraig Feeney	Padraig Mannion
Michael Mulry	Colm Kelly	Brian Mulry
Liam Murray		Ray Mulry
Terry Crowley	Damien Lohan	Brendan Boyle
Teddy Galvin	Pat Regan	Joe Mannion

SUBSTITUTES: Darren Daly for Adrian Tully

GALWAY

BACK ROW L TO R: Eugene Cloonan, Cathal Moore, Joe McGrath, Pat Costello, Tom Helebert, Joe Rabbitte, William Burke, Brian Feeney;

FRONT ROW L TO R: Justin Campbell, Kevin Broderick, Joe Cooney, Nigel Shaughnessy, Michael Healy, Vinnie Maher, Alan Kerins.

ROSCOMMON
BACK ROW L TO R: Joe Mannion, Liam Murray, Damien Lohan, Ray Mulry, Adrian Tully; Brian Mulry, Padraig Feeney, Michael Mulry;
FRONT ROW L TO R: Teddy Galvin, Pat Regan, Brendan Boyle, Terry Crowley, Padraig Mannion, Marty Healy, Colm Kelly.

SUNDAY, JUNE 22, 1997

ULSTER SENIOR HURLING CHAMPIONSHIP SEMI-FINAL

DOWN versus DERRY

CASEMENT PARK, BELFAST

REFEREE: TOMMY MCINTYRE (ANTRIM)

RESULT: DOWN 1-15 DERRY 1-10

DOWN PRODUCED A STORMING late rally which yielded seven points without reply to eventually overhaul rank outsiders Derry in a game where most of the excitement was confined to the last fifteen minutes.

Down struggled for long periods during the game and it looked bleak for the favourites when All-Star nominee, Oliver Collins, scored 1-2 within eleven minutes of his introduction early in the second-half to edge Derry ahead by two points.

Antrim-born, Frank Dawson, in his first year in charge of the Down team, was a worried man at that stage as Derry threatened to cause a surprise.

"With ten minutes to go in the game, I was standing on the sideline thinking how to address my resignation letter," Frank told me. "But it was then that the true character of the Down team shone through and in a blinding finish, we knocked over seven unanswered points to win a game that was running away from us. The resignation letter stayed in my head and was never printed!"

Down held a two points advantage, 1-5 to 0-6, at the end of an error-ridden first-half of poor quality fare. Martin Coulter Junior scored the opening goal after 22 minutes to push Down 1-4 to 0-3 clear, but Derry hit back with three points from their top scorer, Dermot Kelly, who converted no less than six frees in the first-half.

There was a considerable improvement in the standard of play in the second-half and the closeness of the exchanges ensured interest was kept alive among both sets of supporters.

Oliver Collins, unable to start because of injury, was given a warm welcome when he made a surprise appearance little more than ten minutes after the re-start. Collins made an instant impact with a fine point, and the sharpshooter added a further 1-1 to his tally over the next ten minutes to give Derry a two points advantage.

But in-form wing-back, Martin Coulter Senior, steadied Down's nerves with an excellent point to signal an all-out offensive that simply swept Derry aside.

The Down team came in for some criticism after their lethargic performance, but manager Frank Dawson believes not enough credit was given to Derry for their gutsy display.

"We never got started in this game from midfield up and it was thanks to our defence that we were still in the game at half-time, such was the Derry pressure. The second-half wasn't an awful lot better and Derry took over for a time when Oliver Collins came on as a substitute and scored 1-2. But we finished strongly and scored some great points."

SCORERS - DOWN: Martin Coulter Junior 1-2; Johnny McGrattan 0-3; Martin Coulter Senior 0-3; Martin Bailie 0-2; Noel Sands 0-2; Gary Savage 0-1; Gerard McGrattan 0-1; Barry Coulter 0-1
DERRY: Dermot Kelly 0-6; Oliver Collins 1-2; John Dwyer 0-1; Michael Collins 0-1

DOWN

Graham Clarke

Gerard Adair — Stephen Murray — Barry Smith

Marty Mallon — Michael Braniff — Martin Coulter Senior

Gary Savage — Paul Coulter

Barry Coulter — Martin Bailie — Gerard McGrattan

Martin Coulter Junior — Johnny McGrattan — Noel Sands

SUBSTITUTES: Kevin Coulter for Gerard Adair; Michael Blaney for Johnny McGrattan

DERRY

James Donaghy

Joe Young — Paul McCloy — Adrian Hickey

Niall Mullan — Declan Cassidy — Colm McEldowney

Brendan Ward — Ronan McCloskey

Gregory Biggs — Geoffrey McGonagle — Dermot Kelly

Gary Biggs — Michael Collins — John Dwyer

SUBSTITUTES: Colm McGurk for Niall Mullan; Oliver Collins for Gary Biggs

SUNDAY, JULY 6, 1997

ULSTER SENIOR HURLING CHAMPIONSHIP FINAL

DOWN versus ANTRIM

CASEMENT PARK, BELFAST

REFEREE: PAT HORAN (OFFALY)

RESULT: DOWN 3-14 ANTRIM 0-19

OVERWHELMING FAVOURITES ANTRIM were sent crashing out of the Championship by a Down side that delivered a vastly improved performance from that which saw them struggle to beat Derry in the semi-final. 'Man Of The Match', Noel Sands, one of the few players to distinguish himself against Derry, emerged as Down's scoring hero with a tally of one goal and nine points, while Jackie Carson scored no less than thirteen points for an Antrim team that failed to sparkle on the day.

Down manager Frank Dawson was extremely satisfied that his game-plan worked out so well and that Antrim were caught off-guard.

"The weight of expectation within the county was lifted after our poor display against Derry in the semi-final and many supporters expected us to be beaten by double scores. I decided the team should line-out as per the programme, but on a call from me after one minute, would change to their playing positions leaving just two players, Gerard McGrattan and Martin Coulter, up front. When I called the change, my forwards went everywhere.

I lined out four half-forwards to stop the Antrim half-backs dominating the game and this worked a treat."

If the Down players had difficulty motivating themselves against Derry, there were no such problems for the game against arch rivals Antrim. However, Down suffered a set-back before the start when Kevin Coulter had to withdraw because of a flu virus and Barry Milligan was drafted into the defence. Milligan, Stephen Murray and Barry Smith formed a solid full-back line that thwarted the Antrim attack on numerous occasions. Marty Mallon was outstanding in defence and he was ably assisted by his half-back colleagues, Michael Braniff and Martin Coulter Senior, known to one and all as Tom Coulter. Goalkeeper Graham Clarke never put a foot wrong and brought off two wonderful saves in the first-half as Antrim fought desperately for that vital goal.

Noel Sands gave Down the lead inside the first minute with a fine goal to set the trend for the remainder of the game. Sands, who played at midfield after his opening goal, ran himself to a standstill and produced a stunning display of positive hurling. Jackie Carson kept Antrim in touch in the early stages with some excellent free-taking, but a well-taken Barry Coulter goal after 23 minutes pushed Down 2-5 to 0-5 ahead.

Sands accounted for 1-4 as Down built up a five points lead, 2-8 to 0-9, by half-time. Carson scored seven points for Antrim in that opening half to keep the defending champions well in touch.

"Going in five points in front at half-time was a bonus, even though we were facing the breeze in the second-half," Frank Dawson commented. "I told the players it was all down to self-belief and that they had the ability to win the game. It was just a matter of wanting it badly enough."

Former All-Star Gerard McGrattan scored Down's third goal early in the second-half, but with Carson displaying unerring accuracy from frees, Antrim battled back bravely and had reduced the margin to a single point entering the final ten minutes. This was a crucial period of the game, but the expected Antrim take-over never materialised. Instead, Noel Sands converted three frees in the closing stages to seal a well-deserved victory.

Down manager, Frank Dawson, was somewhat concerned when Antrim began to claw their way back, but was proud of the way his team responded to the challenge.

"I was delighted with the manner of our victory as the team displayed a brand of hurling way above expectations. I sat the next morning and watched the Munster Hurling Final with no great interest, until I suddenly realised that we would be playing Tipperary in the All-Ireland Quarter-Final. The following night, I met the team at training and discussed the game against Antrim and the forthcoming clash with Tipperary."

SCORERS - DOWN: Noel Sands 1-9; Gerard McGrattan 1-3; Barry Coulter 1-0; Gary Savage 0-1; Marty Mallon 0-1
ANTRIM: Jackie Carson 0-13; Gregory O'Kane 0-2; Conor McCambridge 0-1; Aidan Mort 0-1; Aidan Delargy 0-1; Alastair Elliot 0-1

DOWN

Graham Clarke

Barry Smith | Stephen Murray | Barry Milligan
Marty Mallon | Michael Braniff | Martin Coulter Senior

Gary Savage | Paul Coulter

Barry Coulter | Martin Bailie | Gerard McGrattan
Martin Coulter Junior | Jerome McCrickard | Noel Sands

SUBSTITUTES: Brian Braniff for Jerome McCrickard

ANTRIM

Shane Elliot

Ciaran McCambridge | Eoin Colgan | Seán McIlhatton
Sean Paul McKillop | Gary O'Kane | Paul Jennings

Jim Connolly | Paul McKillen

Conor McCambridge | Gregory O'Kane | Aidan Mort
Aidan Delargy | Jackie Carson | Alastair Elliot

SUBSTITUTES: Terence McNaughton for Paul Jennings;
Jim Close for Aidan Delargy; Joe Boyle for Gregory O'Kane

DOWN

BACK ROW L TO R: Frank Dawson (Manager), Jerome McCrickard, Gerard McGrattan, Gary Savage, Barry Coulter, Stephen Murray, Graham Clarke, Barry Milligan, Martin Bailie;
FRONT ROW LTO R: Barry Smith, Noel Sands, Martin Coulter (Junior), Michael Braniff, Martin Coulter (Senior), Marty Mallon, Paul Coulter.

ANTRIM

BACK ROW L TO R: John Carson, Aidan Mort, Ciaran McCambridge, Paul Jennings, Seán McIlhatton, Gary O'Kane, Seán Paul McKillop;
FRONT ROW L TO R: Conor McCambridge, Jim Connolly, Eoin Colgan, Paul McKillen, Shane Elliot, Gregory O'Kane, Alastair Elliot, Aidan Delargy

SATURDAY, JULY 26, 1997

ALL-IRELAND SENIOR HURLING QUARTER-FINAL

TIPPERARY versus DOWN

ST. TIGHEARNACH'S PARK, CLONES

REFEREE: DICKIE MURPHY (WEXFORD)

RESULT: TIPPERARY 3-24 DOWN 3-8

BEATEN MUNSTER FINALISTS Tipperary got back on the winning trail and easily qualified for an All-Ireland semi-final tilt against defending champions Wexford after disposing of the Down challenge with consummate ease. Clones was an unlikely setting for an All-Ireland hurling quarter-final, but the unfamiliar surroundings failed to distract Len Gaynor's men from their task at hand. Tipperary dominated the game throughout and led at one stage by no less than twenty points, but three goals for Down in the closing stages served to put some semblance of respectability on the scoreboard.

Down manager, Frank Dawson, encouraged by the successes against both Derry and Antrim, felt his side had a reasonable chance coming into the game, but Tipperary proved far too strong on the day.

"I decided that Gary Savage would play on Paul Shelly at corner-back and bring him out the field. This ploy worked to a certain extent, but then Shelly decided to stay back and play as a sweeper. It was important that we be in contention at half-time to have any chance, but the twelve points gap made our task impossible. I asked my players at half-time to go out and give their all in the second-half and in fairness I felt they did themselves justice by scoring three goals."

John Leahy scored eight points for Tipperary and clearly demonstrated why he is one of the most skilful players in the game with a devastating display of power hurling.

Down started in promising fashion, but their challenge disintegrated when Eugene O'Neill scored the opening goal to leave Tipperary 1-3 to 0-2 ahead after 13 minutes play. Down could only muster two further points for the reamainder of the half while Tipperary scored ten points to put the game way beyond the reach of the Ulster Champions at the half-way stage.

Aidan Ryan replaced the injured Kevin Tucker at half-time and marked his return by scoring a splendid goal. When John Leahy landed his sixth point with less than a quarter of an hour remaining, Tipperary had surged ahead by some twenty points, 2-20 to 0-6, and were cruising to an All-Ireland semi-final showdown with reigning champions, Wexford.

Former All-Star, Gerard McGrattan, Barry Coulter and Noel Sands scored a goal each for Down in the last quarter to take the lop-sided look off the scoreline. Sands doubled on the ball to score the most spectacular goal of the Championship. Portaferry clubman Sands is a supremely gifted player.

Before the game had run its inevitable course, substitute Aidan Flanagan scored a well-taken goal and Leahy rounded off the scoring with a fine point. Nine Tipperary players found the target in an all too one-sided encounter.

SCORERS - TIPPERARY: John Leahy 0-8; Thomas Dunne 0-5; Aidan Ryan 1-2; Aidan Flanagan 1-1; Brian O'Meara 0-3; Liam McGrath 0-3; Eugene O'Neill 1-0; Liam Cahill 0-1; Kevin Tucker 0-1
DOWN: Noel Sands 1-4; Gerard McGrattan 1-1; Barry Coulter 1-0; Gary Savage 0-2; Michael Braniff 0-1

TIPPERARY

Brendan Cummins

Paul Shelly   Noel Sheehy   Michael Ryan

Liam Sheedy   Colm Bonnar   Brendan Carroll

Thomas Dunne   Conor Gleeson

Kevin Tucker   Liam McGrath   John Leahy

Liam Cahill   Eugene O'Neill   Brian O'Meara

SUBSTITUTES: Aidan Ryan for Kevin Tucker; Aidan Flanagan for Eugene O'Neill; Aidan Butler for Colm Bonnar

DOWN

Graham Clarke

Kevin Coulter   Stephen Murray   Barry Milligan

Marty Mallon   Michael Braniff   Martin Coulter Senior

Gary Savage   Paul Coulter

Martin Coulter Junior   Martin Bailie   Gerard McGrattan

Noel Sands   Jerome McCrickard   Barry Coulter

SUBSTITUTES: Brian Braniff for Martin Bailie; John McGrattan for Martin Coulter Junior

TIPPERARY

BACK ROW L TO R: Noel Sheehy, Brian O'Meara, Conor Gleeson, Brendan Cummins, Brendan Carroll, Thomas Dunne, Liam Sheedy;

FRONT ROW L TO R: Liam McGrath; Michael Ryan, Colm Bonnar, Kevin Tucker; Paul Shelly, John Leahy, Eugene O'Neill, Liam Cahill.

DOWN
BACK ROW L TO R: Jerome McCrickard, Gary Savage, Stephen Murray, Barry Coulter, Martin Bailie, Kevin Coulter, Gerard McGrattan;
FRONT ROW L TO R: Noel Sands, Paul Coulter, Martin Coulter (Senior), Marty Mallon, Michael Braniff, Barry Milligan, Martin Coulter (Junior), Graham Clarke

SUNDAY, JULY 27, 1997

ALL-IRELAND SENIOR HURLING QUARTER-FINAL

KILKENNY versus GALWAY

SEMPLE STADIUM, THURLES

REFEREE: PAT O'CONNOR (LIMERICK)

RESULT: KILKENNY 4-15 GALWAY 3-16

THIS WAS DJ CAREY'S DAY! Gowran's hurling wizard inspired Kilkenny's truly remarkable second-half rally with the finest individual display of the '97 Hurling Championship. Carey illuminated the game with his silken skills and clearly underlined just why he is the most outstanding forward in present day hurling.

Consider the facts! Kilkenny trailed by nine points at the interval and their first-half display hardly suggested a comeback of such gigantic porportions. But no one can ever discount a team that includes such a lethal marksman as DJ Carey. The mere mention of his name is sufficient in itself to send a shiver down the spine of the most seasoned defender. Carey had scored a very creditable 1-2 in the opening half but then lifted his game to new heights after the break with a dazzling display that yielded a further 1-6 to dash Galway's hopes. It was a highly competitive and hugely entertaining game that produced top quality hurling and some magnificent scores.

After an early exchange of points, Galway, minus the injured Joe Rabbitte, soon forged ahead after a long-range free from Cathal Moore was finished to the net with a touch from Joe Cooney. That goal proved a launching pad for the Galway team. Moore was commanding at centre-half-back; Justin Campbell and Kevin Broderick exposed deficiencies in the Kilkenny back-line, while Liam Burke won an increasing amount of possession at midfield. Burke scored Galway's second goal after goalkeeper Adrian Ronan lost possession. Carey's first goal was sheer class. He gathered the ball from Michael Phelan before storming through to rifle a shot past Pat Costello.

Galway finished the half more strongly and their cause was further boosted when Kevin Broderick scored a fine goal to leave Kilkenny in near disarray.

Galway held a nine points lead at half-time, 3-9 to 1-6, and few held out any hopes of a Kilkenny revival. Nicky Brennan laid it on the line for his players at half-time and their response was quite magnificent.

Kilkenny made full use of the breeze in the second-half and the Galway defence came under increasing pressure. John Power, who replaced Peter Barry at half-time, had a huge influence on the game. He ignited the Kilkenny challenge. Carey pointed two frees; Andy Comerford sent over a side-line cut and Charlie Carter scored a point from play. Suddenly Galway were vulnerable. Comerford and Philip Larkin were on top at midfield; the full-back line was assured and confident and Pat O'Neill was dominant at centre-half-back. Carey's second goal 11 minutes after the re-start brought Kilkenny to within a point of Galway. Kevin Broderick replied with a point for the League Champions but Michael Phelan then kicked the ball to the net and Carey added a point to leave Kilkenny 3-12 to 3-10 ahead.

Galway rallied and even forged ahead with three unanswered points from the in-form Broderick, Eugene Cloonan and Francis Forde. Substitute Ken O'Shea scored Kilkenny's fourth goal with his first touch after being set up by Carey. That proved the decisive score of the game!

Thereafter, Galway battled bravely to retrieve the game but DJ was in no mood to have his day spoiled. He scored yet another superb point from play and converted a magnificent free in injury-time. It was DJ Carey's day alright. A hurling genius!

SCORERS - KILKENNY: DJ Carey 2-8; Michael Phelan 1-1; Andy Comerford 0-3; Ken O'Shea 1-0; Canice Brennan 0-2; Charlie Carter 0-1
GALWAY: Kevin Broderick 1-4; Eugene Cloonan 0-4; Francis Forde 0-3; Justin Campbell 0-3; Liam Burke 1-0; Joe Cooney 1-0; Cathal Moore 0-1; Alan Kerins 0-1

KILKENNY

Adrian Ronan

Eddie O'Connor — Liam Simpson — Willie O'Connor
Liam Keoghan — Pat O'Neill — Dan O'Neill
Philip Larkin — Andy Comerford
Peter Barry — Canice Brennan — DJ Carey
P.J. Delaney — Michael Phelan — Charlie Carter

SUBSTITUTES: John Power for Peter Barry;
Ken O'Shea for P.J. Delaney; Brian McEvoy for Michael Phelan

GALWAY

	Pat Costello	
Finbar Gantley	William Burke	Brian Feeney
Nigel Shaughnessy	Cathal Moore	Vinnie Maher
Liam Burke		Francis Forde
Justin Campbell	Joe McGrath	Kevin Broderick
Alan Kerins	Joe Cooney	Eugene Cloonan

SUBSTITUTES: Padraig Kelly for Nigel Shaugnessy;
Michael Coleman for Joe McGrath

KILKENNY
BACK ROW L TO R: Dan O'Neill, Philip Larkin, Andy Comerford, Canice Brennan, Michael Phelan, Liam Simpson, Peter Barry, Pat O'Neill;
FRONT ROW L TO R: Eddie O'Connor, Liam Keoghan, DJ Carey, Adrian Ronan, Charlie Carter, P.J. Delaney, Willie O'Connor.

GALWAY
BACK ROW L TO R: Eugene Cloonan, Joe McGrath, Justin Campbell, Cathal Moore, Pat Costello, Brian Feeney, Finbar Gantley, Liam Burke;
FRONT ROW L TO R: William Burke, Kevin Broderick, Nigel Shaughnessy, Joe Cooney, Francis Forde, Alan Kerins, Vinnie Maher.

SUNDAY, AUGUST 10, 1997

ALL-IRELAND SENIOR HURLING SEMI-FINAL

CLARE versus KILKENNY

CROKE PARK

REFEREE: DICKIE MURPHY (WEXFORD)

RESULT: CLARE 1-17 KILKENNY 1-13

A GOOD START is half the battle! That maxim rang true at Croke Park as Clare powered off the blocks and were never once behind in a game they dominated for long periods. Jamesie O'Connor chose the occasion to demonstrate his enormous talent and his nine points tally underlined his massive contribution to Clare's victory. Jamesie also set up numerous other scores and earned the admiration of everyone for his sheer work-rate and utter determination. He combined pace, positioning and accuracy in a vintage display that epitomised everything that was positive about Clare's performance. All around the field Clare won many of the individual battles while once again Brian Lohan was a colossus at full-back. Liam Doyle and Anthony Daly were also very effective in defence.

Kilkenny suffered a severe setback before the start as both Liam Simpson and Michael Phelan were forced to withdraw because of hamstring injuries and were replaced by John Costello and Ken O'Shea, who had scored the decisive goal against Galway in the quarter-final.

Clare, too, had to make an enforced change. Niall Gilligan was called into the side to replace the injured Fergus Tuohy.

Clare began in confident fashion and got through for some early scores. DJ Carey uncharacteristally mis-hit an early free and the clearance from Brian Lohan was gathered by Jamesie O'Connor who laid on the pass for Ger O'Loughlin who shot over a splendid point from a difficult angle. Jamesie O'Connor followed up with a well-taken point before Ger 'Sparrow' O'Loughlin struck for a Clare goal. Fergal Hegarty's shot was blocked by Kilkenny goalkeeper Adrian Ronan and 'Sparrow' finished the rebound to the net. The highly impressive Philip Larkin replied with a point for Kilkenny but Clare continued to press forward and had built up a comfortable 1-5 to 0-2 lead by the tenth minute. Kilkenny rallied with a point each from Charlie Carter, DJ Carey and Pat O'Neill to reduce the margin to just two points.

DJ Carey's powerfully struck penalty was brilliantly saved by Davy Fitzgerald after 26 minutes to thwart Kilkenny efforts to turn the tide. Despite missing a number of good scoring chances, Clare still led at half-time by 1-8 to 0-6 and that margin had been increased to ten points after 45 minutes through some splendid scores from Niall Gilligan, Jamesie O'Connor and P.J. O'Connell.

As the game entered the final quarter, Kilkenny began their fightback in earnest spurred on by a truly superb goal from DJ Carey after an electrifying burst took him past Anthony Daly. Carey could well have scored another goal immediately afterwards, but he was pulled down by Frank Lohan. DJ converted the free himself to bring Kilkenny to within six points of Clare. Jamesie O'Connor then replied with a point for Clare.

Kilkenny produced a storming finish which yielded three points without reply and suddenly the margin was down to four and the Clare defence was under siege. But when the need was greatest, Seán McMahon rose to the challenge and his timely clearances deprived Kilkenny of vital scores.

Mighty Clare were back in an All-Ireland Hurling Final for the second time in three years, while Kilkenny became the first team to lose two Championship games in the one year!

SCORERS - CLARE: Jamesie O'Connor 0-9; Ger O'Loughlin 1-1; Seán McMahon 0-2; P.J. O'Connell 0-2; Niall Gilligan 0-2; David Forde 0-1
KILKENNY: DJ Carey 1-6; Charlie Carter 0-2; Canice Brennan 0-1; Philip Larkin 0-1; Pat O'Neill 0-1; Denis Byrne 0-1; Peter Barry 0-1

CLARE

Davy Fitzgerald

Michael O'Halloran — Brian Lohan — Frank Lohan
Liam Doyle — Sean McMahon — Anthony Daly
Ollie Baker — Colin Lynch
Jamesie O'Connor — Conor Clancy — PJ O'Connell
Niall Gilligan — Ger O'Loughlin — Fergal Hegarty

SUBSTITUTES: David Forde for Fergal Hegarty; Eamonn Taaffe for Ollie Baker

KILKENNY

Adrian Ronan

John Costello — Eddie O'Connor — Willie O'Connor
Dan O'Neill — Pat O'Neill — Liam Keoghan
Philip Larkin — Andy Comerford
John Power — Canice Brennan — DJ Carey
Ken O'Shea — P.J. Delaney — Charlie Carter

SUBSTITUTES: Peter Barry for Ken O'Shea;
Denis Byrne for John Power; Brian McEvoy for Canice Brennan

CLARE
BACK ROW L TO R: Brian Lohan, Michael O'Halloran, Frank Lohan, Colin Lynch, Davy Fitzgerald, Conor Clancy, Ger O'Loughlin, Seán McMahon;
FRONT ROW L TO R: Liam Doyle, Ollie Baker, Anthony Daly, Jamesie O'Connor, P.J. O'Connell, Fergal Hegarty, Niall Gilligan.

KILKENNY
BACK ROW L TO ROW: Dan O'Neill, Philip Larkin, Andy Comerford, John Power, Adrian Ronan, Canice Brennan, John Costello, Pat O'Neill;
FRONT ROW L TO R: Eddie O'Connor, Liam Keoghan, P.J. Delaney, DJ Carey, Charlie Carter, Ken O'Shea, Willie O'Connor.

SUNDAY, AUGUST 17, 1997

ALL-IRELAND SENIOR HURLING SEMI-FINAL

TIPPERARY versus WEXFORD

CROKE PARK

REFEREE: JOE O'LEARY (CORK)

RESULT: TIPPERARY 2-16 WEXFORD 0-15

TIPPERARY ARE BACK centre stage and looking good! All-Ireland Champions Wexford suffered the same fate as their football counterparts, Meath, who lost their crown less than twenty-four hours earlier when going down heavily to Offaly in the Leinster Final. Tipperary now play Clare in a first-ever All-Munster, All-Ireland hurling final! The two-year experiment of allowing the beaten provincial finalists in both Munster and Leinster back into the All-Ireland series worked out to near perfection for a completely transformed Tipperary team. The bitter disappointment of their Munster Final defeat by Clare was quickly forgotten as new-look Tipperary took their second chance with a style and panache that was largely absent in the provincial decider. Len Gaynor made sweeping changes to the side that lost by three points against Clare six weeks previously and Tipperary profitted as a consequence.

Wexford's challenge was weakened by an injury to captain Rod Guiney who had to retire after less than five minutes play and their cause was further undermined when John Leahy scored a fine goal for Tipperary when he diverted a high ball from Conor Gleeson into the net. Earlier, Wexford full-forward, Gary Laffan, doubtful before the start because of injury, was denied a goal by the ever vigilant and agile Brendan Cummins. The All-Ireland champions were finding it difficult against a rock solid Tipperary defence that had many outstanding performers, notably Paul Shelly and Colm Bonnar.

But, more than anyone else, it was Leahy, despite suffering a serious jaw injury, who was responsible for Tipperary's early advantage and, apart from the goal, he also scored some fine points to leave his side 1-5 to 0-5 ahead after 24 minutes. By that stage, Wexford had been dealt a further blow when Rory McCarthy suffered concussion after a collision with Conor Gleeson. All-Star McCarthy played on until half-time when he was replaced by Michael Jordan.

Tipperary's second goal came about after Leahy forced a great save from Fitzhenry, only for Brian O'Meara to finish the ball to the net. Wexford were struggling to penetrate the Tipperary back-line and relied heavily on the impressive Paul Codd to keep them in touch with points from play and frees.

Tipperary held a six points advantage at half-time, 2-7 to 0-7, but with Martin Storey now operating at full-forward, Wexford staged a revival of sorts. Paul Codd and Tommy Dunne exchanged points but Storey was now making an impact. The Oulart-The-Ballagh player landed two points from play in quick succession to reduce the margin to four points. Declan Ryan replied with a point for Tipperary and that pattern was repeated on no less than four occasions over the next twenty minutes. Everytime Wexford got the margin down to four points, Tipperary responded with a point of their own to keep the champions at arms' length.

Still, the Wexford defence, particularly the half-back line, proved strong and resilient in the second-half, but their forward colleagues squandered many good scoring chances. All-Star Liam Cahill replaced Eugene O'Neill while Aidan Ryan came on for the injured John Leahy and both men played their part in Tipperary's victory.

Billy Byrne made his customary appearance for Wexford, but this time there was no 'golden' goal for the super-sub. Michael Cleary had an excellent last quarter and his two points in the closing stages, supplemented by one each from Liam Cahill and Brian O'Meara, pushed Tipperary eight points clear. Paul Codd landed his eighth point for Wexford near the very end but, all in all, not a happy day for the champions, who learned all about the hazards of defending an All-Ireland crown.

Full credit to Tipperary, who became the first team to reach the All-Ireland final as a result of the 'second chance' loophole and now play Munster Champions Clare in a unique hurling decider.

SCORERS - TIPPERARY: John Leahy 1-4; Thomas Dunne 0-4; Brian O'Meara 1-1; Michael Cleary 0-3; Conor Gleeson 0-1; Declan Ryan 0-1; Liam Cahill 0-1; Liam McGrath 0-1
WEXFORD: Paul Codd 0-8; Martin Storey 0-3; Larry Murphy 0-1; Liam Dunne 0-1; Michael Jordan 0-1; Tom Dempsey 0-1

TIPPERARY

Brendan Cummins

Paul Shelly — Noel Sheehy — Michael Ryan

Liam Sheedy — Colm Bonnar — Conal Bonnar

Thomas Dunne — Conor Gleeson

Liam McGrath — Declan Ryan — John Leahy

Michael Cleary — Eugene O'Neill — Brian O'Meara

SUBSTITUTES: Liam Cahill for Eugene O'Neill;
Aidan Ryan for John Leahy

WEXFORD

Damien Fitzhenry

Colm Kehoe — Ger Cush — Eugene Furlong

Rod Guiney — Liam Dunne — Sean Flood

Adrian Fenlon — Larry O'Gorman

Rory McCarthy — Martin Storey — Larry Murphy

Paul Codd — Gary Laffan — Tom Dempsey

SUBSTITUTES: John O'Connor for Rod Guiney;
Michael Jordan for Rory McCarthy; Billy Byrne for Larry Murphy

TIPPERARY
BACK ROW L TO R: Thomas Dunne, Noel Sheehy, Brendan Cummins, Conor Gleeson, Brian O'Meara,
FRONT ROW L TO R: Michael Cleary, Eugene O'Neill, Colm Bonnar, Michael Ryan, Paul Shelly, John Leahy, Declan Ryan, Conal Bonnar.

WEXFORD
BACK ROW L TO R: Larry O'Gorman, Rod Guiney, Adrian Fenlon, Larry Murphy, Gary Laffan, Ger Cush, Eugene Furlong;
FRONT ROW L TO R: Liam Dunne, Seán Flood, Damien Fitzhenry, Martin Storey, Tom Dempsey, Paul Codd, Colm Kehoe, Rory McCarthy.